To Sue,

With very &

"Grandad" !

May, 2022

DIARY OF A GRANDAD - PLUS!

FOR THE GRANDCHILDREN,

and in memory of

JAMES D. HEGARTY (1976-2020)

DIARY OF A GRANDAD - PLUS!

THE SECOND EDITION OF "DIARY OF A GRANDAD"

JOHN HEGARTY

Paperback Edition First Printing, 2022

Published by Clayhanger Press under their
TERTIUS INGPEN imprint.
7 Highfield Court
Newcastle under Lyme
Staffordshire
ST5 3LT
www.clayhangerpress.co.uk

ISBN 9798780581611

TERTIUS INGPEN

ACKNOWLEDGEMENTS

Of course, this diary could not have been written without the stars of the show, our grandchildren: Daniel, Callum, Ellie, Aimee, and Charlotte. Thank you to you all for lovely times together and many happy memories.

They were eagle-eyed when spotting silly mistakes but Helen, my cousin on my mother's side, was a hero in volunteering to go through the final draft. She spotted all sorts of inconsistencies; the errors in the final version are my responsibility alone.

Roger Bloor, and his publishing house Clayhanger Press, tirelessly saw the first edition through to publication and has encouraged me with this second edition - which features additional material originated by the five grandchildren for initial publication in the Ashley Parish Magazine, Ashley Parish Church, Staffordshire.

My wife Rosie, and many people, too numerous to remember, have encouraged me in the writing of "Diary of a Grandad" over nearly a decade, and their suggestions to write this collection, have kept me at it. Thanks to you all!

INTRODUCTION

Why?

I edit the Ashley Parish Magazine, the monthly newsletter of Ashley Parish Church, Staffordshire. It is a delight to put together items of church news with articles from parishioners.

But I find myself often short of material to fill the monthly pages. I must have seen somewhere in the national press "Diary of a Grandad", and I thought – I could do that!

So, with the ongoing support of our five grandchildren: Charlotte, Ellie, Aimee, Callum and Daniel, I have shared stories of little adventures and gatherings we have had together at our farm, where we are fortunate all to live together in our separate houses with a common yard, or patio if one is posh.

But I was not alone in featuring in the monthly "Parish Magazine" with "Diary of a Grandad". No! The grandchildren also contributed with poems (Charlotte and Ellie), and recipes (Aimee, with Callum and Dan, chief tasters). Now, in "Diary of a Grandad – PLUS!" you can read the COMPLETE WORKS of the Blore Heath grand-family.

With thanks to the grandchildren's parents and my wife, Rosie, I hope you enjoy reading these collected stories, poems and recipes which span nearly a decade from 2013 to 2022.

John Hegarty
The Old Dairy, Blore Heath Farm
March 2022

Diary of a Grandad

Poems

Recipes

DIARY OF A GRANDAD

1: Laddering - a new pastime

Your editor is lucky to see his two grandsons and three granddaughters on a daily basis, here at the Blore Heath ranch. It's such fun that he just had to write about some of the wonderful experiences they have given him. We start in April, 2013.

Callum hasn't been all that well lately. He suffers from asthma, and it lays him low. But yesterday he was in fine fettle. He was back from pre-school early; the weather wasn't too bad and C. wanted to

C: "Make a boat please Grandad?"

"What kind of boat?"

C: "One for everyone to ride in on the pond."

"A boat to ride in is not easy to make C., what about a model boat?"

(Actually, all Grandad had in mind was putting a stick through a polystyrene food tray with a bit of a sail made of a piece of paper. I had found from previous experience with cub scout events that they not only float but zing across the water with the slightest puff of wind, and beat other, more elaborate constructions.)

Anyhow, by the time we got into the workshop, C. had forgotten about the boat and was into painting, drilling, hammering, sawing, and getting his boots stuck in cow muck. And then he noticed the ladder.

C. is pretty keen on climbing - always has been. He has spent many a happy hour shinning up all sorts of places that really he shouldn't, like the kitchen cabinets, and his brother D. is taking after him.)

C: "Grandad, you need to come with me with the ladder." So we picked up a regular, normal, aluminium ladder and between the two of us set off for the outside. C. insisted we stop at various intervals, and prop the ladder against something, so that he could climb up it. At the top (as far as he dared go) he looked around and admired the view, commenting and delighting in what he could now see (I cannot convey the delight and humour of this in print!).

For about an hour we moseyed around the farm, propping the ladder against the fence, barn wall, hedge, railings and finally - the piles of muck in the field. All chosen of course by C. Before the muck heaps he said (conspiratorially),

"Grandad, I know where we need to go…...and it's really smelly…."

Which of course we did. Home to tea and bed, one very tired grandson…

It occurs to me that C. has invented a brand-new leisure pursuit. In these times of austerity, what could be better than taking a ladder outside, propping it up against whatever takes your fancy and admiring the view. Try it (but better with a young comrade-in-ladders!), best of all, "C."

2: Well, Grandad! And: The Easter story in 60 seconds

Scene 1: Ellie (aged 5) and Charlotte (7) are sitting at table, with their evening meal. Grandad has dropped in to chat and enjoy a small glass of something or other... Mum and Gr. are chatting about odds and ends, including work, when smaller people want to share in the conversation...

Ch: Where do you work Grandad?

Gr: I work at a big school, called a university.

E: What do you do there?

Gr: I am a sort of a teacher, a university teacher.

E: What do you teach?

[Gr has to pause and think - how to convey something about psychology to them -]

Gr: I teach about how the mind works, how people think and feel.

[But this didn't mean much - E and Ch]:   silence

Gr: [has inspired thought and says somewhat smugly]: I teach them how to write … STORIES.

E: [in a voice loaded with irony] Well, Grandad, how old are they? Aren't they ... Adults?

Gr: Yes

E: Well, Grandad, they should KNOW how to write stories...

****

Scene 2: Easter Sunday, about 5.30 pm, family tea. E. is invited to sing some songs, with Daddy accompanying on the guitar. She sings selections from one of her favourite films - Mary Poppins. Daddy then suggests she shares her reaction to the Easter story, heard at school church visit during Holy Week.

E: (centre 'stage', balanced, incidentally, on roller blades):

"Well, do you know, Jesus' friends did a very, very, very mean thing. He rode on a donkey, then they put a holly crown on his head and nailed him to a cross. Then he died [audience sighs]."

"But, but, but ... [reassuringly]… [dramatic pause] ... it was alright. He came alive again. [audience relieved.]

"But … [dramatic pause 2.] ... then he died again."

[Family suggests - went into heaven?]

E: "Yes."

[On a cloud?]

E: "Nah!"

3: Green fingers

Callum (aged 4) does everything at the double. Thankfully he has recovered from a bad period with his asthma and now has the energy of a nuclear reactor. Grandad tries to keep up as C. belts off to the workshop / polytunnel to pursue a project. Today he found an old-fashioned cage-type of rat trap in the shed, wanted to know what it was for, and then decided we had to implement it there and then. (What is it about getting older that you lose that verve, immediacy and vivacity and find yourself saying what you remember your parents - boringly - saying - well, perhaps later… Deep breath, do not say that!)

So, deep breath, I said he needed to have some bait -? - like cattle feed - [pause while thinks] - off at the double to the shed to the sacks of cattle feed concentrate. None open. - ? - I think there is some left over in here … C. - [grabs bucket], "This will do Grandad.". Duly primed, the rat trap goes into C.'s chosen spot … and then on to the next project. (We did not catch anything!)

This is all taking place on a squally day in mid-May. I think they are usually called April showers. They are bad enough even if you have the polytunnel to duck into. Fortunately, it is bolted down to a concrete base with serious scaffolding brackety type things and does not lift off its base like it might do. But the rain makes a powerful racket.

Talking of polytunnels, C. loves planting things. He saw where the seed packets were, and duly appeared with them, sat down, ripped them open [to be fair, he has seen me open them like that, only he did not realise he had to shake the seeds to the bottom and then rip across the top, but we'll let that pass] and shook the seeds onto the concrete.

Then he picked them up one by one, made a little furrow with his finger, dropped them in, patted the soil down, and then had me fill the watering can (he cannot lift it up to the tap although he tries to) so that he could drench them with water (no, gently, C.!). I think he has green fingers because they have grown. We have a single broad bean plant in the polytunnel where he put it, and some radishes in a little furrow where he put those.

Later on, the radishes were red enough to harvest, so he took them in to Mum who said they were lovely. C. eschewed them - too extreme food for a pre-schooler?

4: Industry-scale plant production

This episode features Callum's sister, Aimee, (age 6), who took a fancy to doing some gardening…

Grandad was pricking out some seedlings into a tray, when A. thought she would like to do this too.

She got the idea pretty quickly. Get a pot, get a seed tray to put the pot in, put some potting compost in it, put a seed in, cover it up, write a label…job done. Gr. has to admit that he thought she would lose interest pretty quickly.

But, no! She diligently worked through every packet of seeds Grandad had, periodically coming for another tray, more pots, more potting compost, labels, until there was a veritable forest of pots, each with a neatly-written plant label. To make things easier for her, I set up a little work-station with an upturned crate, to which she added an upturned large flower-pot for a seat.

Towards the end of the afternoon, A.'s cousins arrived on the scene and of course wanted to join in. So I now had three enthusiastic helpers and an ever-growing acreage of pots.

Dedicated readers of this series will no doubt be wondering where Callum was in all of this. Well, he was doing his own thing elsewhere in the garden sowing a packet of peas he had spirited away, unknown and unseen by the girls.

Fast-forward a few weeks, and I am looking out now on the results of this sowing-party. We've got all sorts of wonderful things coming on - hollyhocks, tomatoes, cauliflowers, lettuce…and a mysterious pot of what are probably sunflowers, labelled "Teddy Bears" (possibly because it was a "children's" packet with teddy bears on it!). C's special area has a little plot of peas growing nicely.

The Factory Shop in 'Drayton has a special offer on plant containers made out of a strong fabric (like barbeque covers) so I am going to get some to make vegetable beds that A. and team can plant up and which are "hers". I'll report on the harvest in due course.

5: Have wheels, will travel

Callum was moodling in the workshop with me, and he sat on the mobility scooter which had belonged to my stepmother, Eleanor. He did not know what it did! [Hah-hah! The power of being an adult!] Deeming he was now old enough, I said, turn that key, and push that lever (I had turned the speed knob to the lowest setting, note!). So, it moved!!!!!

Well, of course you can imagine the excitement. Then we had about half an hour of C. manoeuvring the scooter backwards and forward inside one of our farm buildings and generally getting the feel of how to start and stop and turn. Moreover, he soon got the idea of three-point turns.   (Actually, if you think about it, mobility scooters are ideal for youngsters as they have bicycle-like handlebars, and a low centre of gravity, four wheels rather than two, and an automatic brake - in fact, safer than a bike! Of course you need safe, flat space to ride it on….and one that won't go too fast.

Avid followers of this column will guess that half an hour was only a warm-up - and so it was. Having got the idea of how it all worked, C. wanted to take the scooter outside. We fashioned some simple ramps from old pieces of wood to negotiate the ups and downs of our building levels and thus C. emerged. like a butterfly out of a chrysalis, onto our concrete drive.

C. soon found the speed control and thus took off at about 4mph. I had to laugh when he turned too fast, spun himself off and ran round and round, holding the handlebars, whilst the vehicle went in circles! He realised he could jump on and off whilst at speed, so all was well.

Since then, the youngsters have had a ball. Not only C., but all our other grandchildren and their guests have really, really enjoyed Eleanor's bequest. They have invented all sorts of games with it, been pretty good at sharing turns, and can be often seen just cruising around, enjoying the experience! Sometimes they even allow the oldies to have a go.

By the way, how many children can you get on such a scooter? (Answers on a postcard please.)

6: Mud, mud, glorious mud

A legacy of the former gravel workings at the farm is a pond. The water level varies from almost nothing to very overflowing, depending on rainfall. The past few months, being relatively dry, has meant the slow disappearance of a lot of the water, leaving behind various thicknesses of a silt and water mixture. Whatever its technical name, it's … mud.

Now Callum (aged four) has always liked natural textures. He loves to run his hands through piles of stones, or to scoop up soil. The other day we set out on an expedition to the pond. C. led the way ("I know how to get there with no brambles, Grandad!"). It worked and we arrived, pond-side, unscratched.

There are two necessary aspects to pond investigation. One is to walk on a muddy bit ("Be careful you don't sink, C!") with a view to seeing how deep it is. Actually this is quite thrilling, because you do not necessarily know in advance how likely you are to sink a little bit or a lot. I mean, we are not talking quagmires here, no Grimpen Mire (for Hound of the Baskervilles aficionados) that can swallow mules and prison escapees, but I (Grandad) have actually sunk so deep I could not pull my welly boot out (which is a bit embarrassing). The other aspect (i.e., for C.) is to plunge one's hands into the ooze and slime, lift handfuls and let it slither through one's fingers. Readers with a similar interest might wish to share the joys of this on another postcard please. Sometimes we bring buckets of it back so the other grandchildren can enjoy the delights of this mud in the comfort of their own back yard.

Another expedition, this time with C.'s Dad, and brother Daniel, took place last weekend. Now I personally prefer to wear work gloves with vinyl palms when working outside so I had a pair tucked into my pockets. D. watched his brother oozing and sliming and throwing stones into the water and decided he wanted to do that too. But D. does not like to feel his hands dirty. So, in a stroke of genius I thought, he pulled my gloves out of my pockets and had me put them on him. Obviously, they were a bit too big, to say the least, but he found them just to his liking and enjoyed digging up muddy stones and chucking them in with big splashes, just like his brother. When we got home, he took them off and gave me them back.

He might have washed them first, but he's only just 2, so I forgave him.

13

7: Wise people send kingly gift at Christmas…

It's always nice when relatives bring back little presents from their holidays. It's sort of a recompense for not being able to be there with them, and nice to be thought of whilst they were away.

And thus it was that a little parcel appeared *chez nous*, from relatives who had been visiting friends in Oman. Can readers guess what it might have had in it? You can have three guesses…

So you might be thinking of … dates?

No.

Or … figs?

No.

Or a stuffed toy camel?

No!

I will have to help you with a clue. Think of the Three Wise Men. You can have three more guesses, and possibly one of them will be spot-on….

Gold?

Don't be daft - who is going to send gold! OK you can have more guesses.

Myrrh?

You are on the right track now, but no.

So it's got to be Frankincense?

Well, actually, yes. We had a little bag of frankincense and a piece of charcoal to burn it on. The leaflet with it ("Frankincense - the gift of Kings") explains that it is tapped from the small, drought-hardy Boswellia tree by slashing the bark and allowing the milky sap to bleed out. The sap then dries in the sun to produce hard resin lumps called "tears". It had been hand-harvested from ancient trees in Dhofar, the southernmost province of the Sultanate of Oman. Apparently, the area has traded incense for over 5000 years. Frankincense was highly prized and used in medicine and religious practices. It is used in Asian medicine to treat digestive conditions and skin complaints. It is suggested that burning incense regularly in the house promotes good health.

It has a lovely smell, although it takes some heat to get it to burn (hence the charcoal). You can get self-lighting charcoal (well, after you have put a flame to it) which spits and crackles like an indoor firework. The crystals produce quite a lot of smoke, and a lot of heat, so you have to be careful what you burn it in.   Oh, and one has to be careful not to trigger the smoke alarms! (That's one thing Mary and Joseph didn't have to worry about.)

8: A 15-foot Christmas Tree? No problem!

Scene: Ashley Church, a few weeks before Christmas.

A churchwarden: "John, do you know where we might get a large Christmas tree for the church?"

And so it was that, one Sunday afternoon, Grandad, grandson C., with his dad and uncle set out for the southern reaches of Blore Heath Farm on the tractor and trailer.

Some years ago, about 10, judging by the rings on the subsequent tree, son-the-younger had planted some Christmas trees. On the edge of the former gravel workings the land is not brilliant, but it benefits from the run-off of a nearby field. Anyhow, those trees had grown wonderfully well - too big for ordinary domestic trees, but brilliant for the bigger building. We were after two - one for Ashley Church, and one for Hales and District Club, where several generations of Hegartys have served on the committee. We were tooled up with sharp saw and rope.

There were several to choose from. C. and his Dad took the tractor round the field to get closer to them, while son-the-elder and Grandad started cutting. It was a bit of a logistical challenge to lift the trees over a hedge but in no time we were loaded up with two trees on the trailer.

Back across the field, a bit wet but then the sun came out. Sitting on the trailer, in the open air, three generations of the family …. special moment!

Grateful thanks to Tony Watson for the next step of the journey, transport and decoration, and the tree was safely installed in the Church.

Time to plant more for a decade ahead!

9: Santa, and painting

With five grandchildren between the ages of 2 and 8, there is a diversity of Santa beliefs.

I confess to often teasing (winding up) the girls in particular (well you have to ready them for the wider world…) So, as Charlotte (8) and Ellie (6) were heading south to maternal grandparents on Christmas Eve, I wondered if they had told Santa that they would not be at home and to deliver the prezzies elsewhere. Quick as a flash, son-the-elder, anxious for no further delays to the departure, said he had emailed Santa to tell him. Ellie accepted this without demur, but Charlotte was sceptical, looked at him most quizzically and questioned. "Did you really?".

I know we all engage in mass deception on the Santa front, but that's an especially tall porky - I mean, how could Santa possibly have the time to check his emails on Christmas Eve...

In the farmhouse, C. was on the ball. He was wrapping up some of his toys, mainly broken ones. "What are you doing, C?" his Dad wanted to know. Answer: "When Santa comes, he can take these away and mend them." A genuinely good idea - it will keep the elves gainfully employed until next year.

[Some time later]

Santa has long since gone and the novelty of the toys is wearing off. Time for some action outside with Grandad.

Knock at the door yesterday. "Can we make something in the workshop Grandad?" C. is into painting. He likes to choose his pots of paint and then he is quite a dab hand at opening them with a screwdriver. Usually he goes for a pot of racing green and some cream for a contrast. He's a bit fussy about brushes and prefers brand new ones if possible (thank goodness for budget brushes at a well-known store). We have some large pieces of left-over foam insulation, which yesterday got a coat of paint.

He makes a pretty good job of his painting, but I still have some work to do to teach him about cleaning the brushes.

10: Let's build a ship

One of the benefits of really wet weather here at Blore Heath is that the ponds fill up. Yes, I know, the continued downpours are definitely not good news for those unfortunate souls in the Somerset Levels, and I feel incredibly sorry for them. But we are in a bit of a rain shadow here and, whilst we get our fair share of wind, we can often be spared the worst of the downpours.

Anyhow, C. was in the mood for adventure. So off he strode down the field, well ahead of us, heading for the wood and the pond. He was as surprised as we were to see the water level massively higher than last week. Quite a decent pond now - you could even row a boat on it. Well, if we had one (see below).

I like to light a fire, so I took paper and dry wood and got a little campfire going. Grandma followed C. around the other side, just making sure he did not fall in in his exuberance for fishing out bits of flotsam. Oh-oh, water deeper than wellies, so a wet-footed C. comes back to campfire.

Various efforts to dry out wet socks to no avail, Grandad unleashes his secret weapon - two pairs of socks, to keep his feet warm in wellies! C. well chuffed to have one of Gr.'s second socks on.

(Digression - these are part of a set of socks "Secret Santa" gave to Grandad last year. 7 pairs of socks, each for one day of week with Monday, Tuesday etc written on them. Thus giving C.'s sister Aimee endless satisfaction in pointing out Grandad has the wrong socks on, on a given day.)

Grandad, in a moment of reverie, says to Grandma, we could row a boat on here now. Actually, we did have one some years ago. Remarkably, I think it was 2007, there was such a lot of rain that the pond level rose dramatically. You can still see the level it rose to by bits of debris lodged in the willow trees around the pond and, incredibly, the area of the pond expanded into the nearby fields to form quite a lake. We actually rowed (yes - rowed, in a boat, with oars) through the gate from one field into the next. The boat is no more; I think it ended up on a carnival float.

C., not behind the door, as my mother used to say, overheard mention of the boat, thus reviving an earlier ambition (see an earlier diary entry). The following day, C., proudly presented me with an intricate (although rather "schematic", as he is only five still) drawing of proposed ship. It has a thing underneath, he pointed out (keel). So, no problem about capsizing then.

11: Art class

Callum and I haven't been doing much this month. He's taken up with school and Grandad has been busy with work and one thing and another. But Mum and Dad had to be off somewhere on a weekday school holiday, so C. came to spend some time *chez* Grandad and Grandma's.

I have found out, since becoming a grandparent, that you never know when you are going to be hosting a visitation of grandchildren. So it pays to get some activities and surprises in stock. On my last visit to stock up (Sue Ryder, Oxfam, Wilkinsons, Factory Shop, Lidl and - a bit further afield - Trago Mills in Falmouth) I had managed to get in a good selection of craft activities, including a really super (and cheap - less than a pound!) "Mosaic Art". They give you different colours of peel-off sticky squares and you prise them off (with some difficulty) and stick them on a picture as per the numbered squares (numbers=colours, get it?). In this case it was a pirate picture with treasure - perfect for C!

So this was pretty good. We spent a good hour peeling off sticky squares. We had quite a production line with me finger-nailing them off and C. putting them on to the picture. Quite clever idea really - as I said, they were numbered by colour, so it was easy to find the right ones (good for colour-blind grandparents).

All good things must come to an end and so what were we going to do next? C. spied pots and tubes of paint in the activity drawer and he really does like painting so that was OK.

Grandad is not very good at fine art really. But to be companionable, he thought he would have a bash. His first painting was of two trees. "That is really good, Grandad."

"Thanks, C!"

C. was doing his own thing. That finished, Grandad thought he would attempt a seascape. Dark sky, breaking waves, sandy beach.

Callum had a look, "Grandad, that doesn't look like anything".

Oh well, back to the drawing board.

18

12: Little happenings

Our lovely grandchildren are getting older (of course!) and so they're changing, little by little. Here are some snapshots of little happenings.

Daniel (aged 2): D. is playing in my car (this is a very special treat). He opens the doors, slams them (fingers are OK so far), invites Grandad to sit in the back (and he must put on his seat belt), sits in the driver's seat, whilst Grandad makes car noises. Grandad gets bored and winds down the passenger seat to almost-horizontal. D. invites Grandad to move from back to passenger seat and Gr. lies down to feign sleep. (Very pleasant, sun shining, quite sleepy actually). Door opens, "Wake up Grandad!"

Callum (now 5): Loves to paint (see last episode). Today, fetches all artist materials from Grandad's special drawer together with large stones from garden (we like stone painting). "Do you want to paint one, Grandad?" Super session ensues, using range of acrylic paints with only two tubes accidentally knelt-upon. Well, patio improved by having large blobs of paint thereupon.

Aimee (now 6): "Cafe" with Grandma. Reads out her menu. Impressive choice that would do any tea shop proud. Soon she will be able to actually cook them - yum yum. (She can make tea already - essential skill.)

Charlotte (8): Off to sleep-over with friends. Bag packed, with no doubt female essentials (dark art to a Grandad.) Has large book under arm (Harry Potter).

Grandad: "What's that for, Charlotte.?"

Ch.: "I need to take this Grandad."

Grandad agrees: note the word, _need_, as in you really cannot have a good time on holiday without a book to read.)

Ellie (7): E loves to sing and dance. Grandad is dragooned into dancing, which is quite keep-fit. Memories of his childhood with family members singing party-pieces and generally having fun. Son-the-elder has remote-controlled hi-fi set-up and E. can choose favourite songs to sing along with and dance to. "Jesus on the Mainline" is popular.

13: Go up there?

Daniel. is two years old and a bit. The miracle of a baby becoming an infant, then a toddler, then a little person is a daily wonder and a delight. So many things to understand, to learn, how to get your own way, how to accommodate other people's wishes, and their emerging language.

All coming to mind the other day. I cannot do justice to it in print, but here goes.

Grandad and Grandma were gardening, up the drive from the homestead. D. was playing with his younger-but-almost-the-same-age cousin, M. We were espied!

"Grandad!", D. shouts. (He has his own words, so this is a translation.) "Go up there?"

This is both a request and a command. He would like to join us in whatever we are doing, but cannot get through the gate, which he knows, and he also understands that there is traffic danger beyond the gate.

The request is repeated, again and again and again, so Grandad knows action is required. He walks down.

"Do you want to come and see what we are doing?" (Yes) "You will have to ask Mummy."

Off he toddles inside his house, apparently asks Mum (Grandad at gate so cannot see). Mummy has apparently agreed (but probably not, see below).

"What about (cousin) M. – does he want to come?"

D. turns to M. Asks him [in his own way but no mistaking – wonderful interchange, just as an adult would, polite, respectful].

D. now with, as he thinks, green light, says to Grandad (again in his own way, but no mistaking). "I need to put on my wellies. But will you stay here at the gate and not move whilst I do so?" Grandad duly waits at gate.

Yikes! Howls of protest emanate from farmhouse. Unbeknownst to Grandad, tea [=supper for some of our posh readers] is on the table and D. is expected to partake. Not what D. had in mind!

Grandad has to do quick summit-style peace negotiation.

"Tell you what, D., how about if we quickly go up to see Grandma and what she is doing and then you come back and have your tea?"

This was acceptable and also M. [cousin, remember?] comes too. Three minutes later, no time for tea to go cold, back in house for super-delectable spread of home-made pizza … **"And chips, Grandad!!"**

14: THWACK!

As I write in my office, I can see out of patio doors on to an area where we are having garden refurbishments. D. (3 years old now!) likes this area. He has watched the builders digging and pickaxing and measuring and trowelling and everything else and spends ages acting it all out again when they are not there. He just quietly gets on with a bit of each, bending down to check levels with the spirit-level, then puts it back against the wall, digging here and there, loading his own little wheelbarrow up - and tipping loads to his own design. It's a delight to watch, and he is really happy in his work.

During this time, big brother C. (5 and a bit) is at school, so D. is king of his domain.

But the other day there was a bit of turf warfare.

It started harmoniously enough, with D. doing his building work. To speed up the process of excavation, D went to get his tractor.

(Digression - this is a lovely toy. It is a tractor that a pre-schooler can sit on and pedal, plus a loader bucket at the front. One can push the bucket into a pile of sand and, admittedly with a bit of difficulty, get loaded up. Then you can lift it and by pulling a handle, tip it all out again. But not only that, there is also a backhoe (excavator) attachment just like a JCB. The only frustrating thing I guess for even a toddler is that there is no engine so it does not quite do the job properly. But back to the story.)

So, D. has mauled said tractor-thingy quite some way from the other end of the garden in order to get some serious work done. As luck would have it, Mum happens to be in Grandad's office watching the little ones at work, and Grandad says, why not video it on his new iPad mini [aren't these great!?]? OK, camera rolling, all is fine and dandy.

Unfortunately, big brother C. decides he wants to use the tractor just as D. has got on it and, regrettably, usurps his little brother physically from the driver's seat.

Now Grandad was not actually watching this unfolding drama as he was busy with editing the Parish Magazine of course. But he did HEAR the younger one's response. Quick as a flash, retribution occurred like a bolt from heaven.

Can you guess how "little" D. responded? Just a clue, he had his spade in his hand at the time (plastic, I hasten to add)…

THWACK!

Filming finished *tout-de-suite* as Mum rushes off to render assistance for sore head with vinegar and brown paper.

15: Very rude God?

Of course you don't know, can never know, what someone else has experienced, has taken in; and specially those of tender years. You are inclined to think they haven't understood, haven't questioned, until ....

It was good to sit down with Ellie (aged 6, about to go into Year 2 at Hugo Meynell) and really, really listen to her. Mum was reassuringly nearby. We were chatting about this and that and then E. said:

E: "Grandad, it is rude, isn't it, when you ask someone a question and they don't answer?"

Grandad: "Yes, E."

E: "Well, then, how is it when you talk to God and he doesn't answer? That is very rude, isn't it?"

Tricky one this, need to have a bit of thinking over that one...seconds hang heavy...

Gr: "I suppose God does not really speak out loud but puts ideas into your head."   (Grandad quite pleased with this.)

E: "Well [E. does long pause, and you can see her thinking], God does not open up your head [demonstrates with hands] and puts something inside, does he? [heavy irony in voice]."

G: "No, He uses your imagination."

E. looks dubious. Grandad embarks on lecture to convey concept of imagination. Something around the idea of - if I was to say I was going to give you a large chocolate bar that was really, really nice could you imagine that in your mind and how you would feel? E. seemed to be reasonably persuaded.

At this point, E. spontaneously sings quite a few verses of several worship songs / hymns, tunefully and from memory. Gr. had never heard them before. Quite amazing and out of the blue.

Well done E. and bravo to all at Hugo Meynell School, where she learned them.

16: Treasure Island

With five grandchildren, birthdays are never far away. And they are always grand occasions. Grandparents get to share in cake, singing "Happy Birthday" and all the fun of watching the presents opened. Why should the children have all the fun? thought Grandad. "I want to have a party this year!" he said to himself. Consultations with senior management seemed not to meet with total approval, but the birthday fairy moves in mysterious ways and, days later, daughter-in-law Caroline queried, what kind of party? Grandad wanted a BBQ at the Blore Heath lido, and plans were laid.

This was all very well, but Grandad wondered what kind of fun could be had over above the scoffing of burgers and crisps with the odd glass of fruit juice thrown in (Grandad himself likes red grape juice). I know, he said to himself, a treasure hunt!

When Grandad was Akela at Ashley Air Scout Group treasure hunts and trails and "wide games" always went down well. Obviously, the treasure had to be buried, and on an island, and there would have to be a treasure map with "X marks the spot". An old tin box, and some chain and a padlock turned up. A trip to town produced chocolate bars (guaranteed treasureful!) and it was easy to bury the box under some bushes on the little island in our pond. Drawing a treasure map was simple. Soaking it in tea, charring the edges and cooking it in the oven produced a sort of wrinkly effect. Rolled up and sealed with wax - perfect!

A lovely day dawned and Grandad returned from church to smells of BBQ and salad laid out (plus fruit juice of course). Soon time for treasure hunt. Map "accidentally" found. Ripped open in excitement.

Obvious where treasure was and everyone ready for expedition to pond. Charlotte, (very on-the-ball, Gr. thought) examined map at some length and pronounced it "not real", as "It's been drawn with felt tips and they are modern". Likely career - forensic scientist?

At pond, water around island no deterrent (only 12 inches deep) and treasure soon found and opened up. Booty shared out. Lovely afternoon weather-wise and everyone enjoys messing around on the beach (well it is, really - pebbly area by water's edge…). Soon time for home.

Wait a minute - where is Callum? And where is remainder of treasure in box?

C. spied wading out to re-bury treasure. Well, a boy never knows when he might get a bit hungry down at the pond on a later date with Grandad.

17: Grandad and Grandma discover Minions

With Summer holidays upon us, and parents needing to be at work, it was a good time for grandparents to be in charge for the odd days. So it was that Charlotte and Ellie appeared bright and early on a Tuesday morning, armed with amusements and entertainments. Ever-watchful for new excitements, Grandad wants to know what's in store for the day's, hopefully fun-packed, programme.

"You might like this DVD, Grandad." proclaimed the younger people.

Gr. has to confess that he had not the faintest idea what *Despicable Me 2* was. He could not remember *Despicable Me 1*, despite being assured he had actually seen it and enjoyed it. With slightly heavy heart [Oh no this might be really boring.], pops the disc into the player and settles down at 9 am. [Did you see that? 9 am – in the morning.]

Now, come on readers, how many of you have heard of these DVDs, the hero, "Gru" and his legion of helper-Minions? Let alone seen either of them! They are cartoons but brilliantly done and voiced by well-known stars.

Space precludes the detailed telling of the story, but Grandad is not ashamed to admit that he has not enjoyed a film as much for ages. He laughed and laughed! (This does not happen often - what is there to laugh about these days on tele - although Mrs Brown's Boys is quite good.)

Gru is a wannabe baddie turned hero. He has three adopted children from *Despicable Me 1* (they got him to adopt them!). As there is no Mrs Gru, his children keep trying to fix him up with a female companion. To help him in his (formerly evil) projects, he has a team of little helpers - "Minions". Then along comes an arch-bad guy who makes them all aggressive with a secret formula potion - but all turns out well in the end and Gru finds his true love in the shape of a James Bond style female accomplice. Great stuff!

Grandma did not miss out because E. and Ch. wanted to make their very own Minions out of felt, so a happy day was spent cutting and sewing. Very presentable, stuffed Minions appeared in due course.

Now Grandad is thinking how to get a legion of Minions to help with all those little jobs around the farm.

18: Party fun and games

Daniel has started school. Proudly he goes with his cousins and brother and sister in a Hugo Meynell uniform, just like them. He hardly seems old enough as he is just 3, but he only does half-days. That gives him quality time with his wheelbarrow, tractor and tool kit before his brother and sister come home. His brother Callum is not altogether pleased with this arrangement of course, as he would like to be home as well. He fears he might be missing something.

As you can imagine, returning from school means some letting off steam. Grandad and Grandma's house has open-plan design so there is quite a bit of floor space. D. asks for the hi-fi to be put on. A trad-jazz CD is favourite at the moment - Clyde Valley Stompers (hands up those who remember them!). Other CDs don't quite cut the mustard for D. He twirls the big volume control knob practically to maximum and starts his own version of body-popping. (Confession - Grandad is not quite sure what this is, so small pause in this article ... whilst he checks out online. OK - it is sort of what D. does, a mixture of acrobatics, disco dancing and punching the air vigorously.) The dance demonstrations are interspersed with running at top speed around all the furniture, Grandad holding his breath that he will not collide with something hard or slip on the lino (actually we don't have lino - we are laminated.) Because the decibel level is making the floor vibrate, not to mention possibly blowing Grandad's hi-fi speakers, surreptitious turning-down happens from time to time. But usually D notices and cranks up the volume again.

Last night was party time for Ellie's 7th birthday. Usual presents and cake and happy birthday etc. And then, something new to Grandma and Grandad - a cardboard donkey full of sweets (picture). It has a Mexican name - pinot, no - piñata! Mum hung it from a convenient beam, produced a small cricket bat, and then the children took it in turns mercilessly to annihilate it, hereupon the sweets fell to the floor and the children shared them out.

Grandad is not totally sure he agrees with socially-condoned cruelty to an animal, albeit one made of cardboard, but I suppose it was good exercise, they knew it was only a game, they were good at taking turns and at sharing out the spoils.

Only thing, Grandad would have quite liked to have a turn.

19: Corn on the cobs

Grandma is away. Relatives had offered her the chance to spend almost a fortnight in the Sultanate of Oman. Doesn't that sound romantic? Grandad was occupied with the start of a new term at Keele Uni. and could not go. He was OK, anyway, reading Lawrence of Arabia - all the sand without the flies! And the desert is in his blood anyway, Great Grandad having spent 3 years in the Western Desert during WW2. "The sand used to get everywhere, John. And the flies – you had to cover your mug with your hand before you could drink your tea."

Emails have come almost as slowly as sea-mail. But they say that Grandma is having the time of her life: riding on a camel, visiting a souk (wondered why she took two large, almost-empty suitcases), and a mosque, camping under the stars, visiting local people. Summer every day. Can't be bad, but what about those flies?

Daniel (aged 3 and a tiny bit) wondered where "Baba" was, because her car was not here. Explained she was on her holidays. A bit later, concerned for Grandad's apparent isolation and general wellbeing, he asked, "When will your mummy be back?" Prickles of tears from Grandad, since his mummy died 45 years ago. Odd, how little things can set you off. Tickled, 'tho, that he spotted the relationship of caring, and the only relationship-concept he could use to explain it was that of "mummy".

Callum was keen to go into the maize field, recently harvested and so just stubble now. Off we went with wheelbarrow and spades. Grandad wondered, what was afoot? Blore Heath wind was blowing as usual ("Blore" = "blewer" (Saxon English) = "blowy") - pretty fresh, needed thick clothing. C. had idea to prospect for treasures.

Grandad must confess here - previous expeditions have in fact yielded small hoards of coins. Funny how discoveries always came when Grandad was standing nearby. This time, C. unearthed various coins - 20p, 2p and a pound. (Later, adult comments about how marvellously clean the coins were escaped C.'s notice, so the excitement remained. But I think he might just suspect something.) Sharp-eyed C. then noticed that at the edge of the field the harvesting machinery had left some maize stalks standing. He raced off, jumping the corn stubble like a mountain goat. Satisfying ten minutes ensued, breaking off the corn cobs and piling them into the wheelbarrow.

"What shall we do with these, C?"   "Feed them to the hens, Grandad."

A good idea, and the hens were well pleased with their very own corn-on-the-cobs!

20: Christmassy thing

It's the run-up to Christmas. Daniel (still not very old) goes to visit Santa.

Santa: "What do you want for Christmas?" D. has his heart firmly on a tractor, what he calls a "Brm-brm". D. tells Santa quite firmly that's what he wants. Time to go. Santa gives present from sack. D. miffed and indignant - "Where's my brm-brm?" Well, Santa did ask him what he wanted.

The Ashley church Christmas tree is resplendent, as usual, big thanks to Tony Watson. Grandad is proud to say that he was part of the home team that went to fetch it from the distant slopes of Blore Heath Farm (see also diary entry no.8). It was a great boys' day out. With adults driving the tractor and in charge of the chainsaw, Callum and Daniel (and Grandad) loved to be tucked safely onto the trailer for a voyage over the fields. Recent rain made for a squelchy passage but we got there without being bogged down.

Christmas tree plantings by son-the-younger (James) some years ago had produced some lovely trees. Soon the chosen ones were hoisted up on to the forks of the tractor and lashed to the trailer. Back to the farmstead. Deep hole dug for one outside "Oak Tree Barn", one despatched to Hales and District Club and of course the Ashley Church one set aside for collection and subsequent installation by Tony W.

Christmas is ever-nearer. Grandad decides to go to the Hugo Meynell School Christmas services at church. Wow! Usually the church has plenty of spare seats. Not today. Seats are moved so every youngster can see Doug leading a special service. Fantastic to see the church overflowing with young people.

The Chapter House is an "angel base" manned by wonderful adult volunteers. Fold A4 sheets fan-wise and with a bit of glue and some printouts - lovely angels. Other Hugo-Meynellers are in the church counting angels. How many are there in the windows, monuments and elsewhere? Come on, regular church-goers, how many?

All five of Grandad's grand-youngsters are there at the Monday and Tuesday services. Aimee and her friend spot the plaque on the piano. "Who was 'Eleanor Hegarty', Grandad?" I explain about step-mum and "Great-Grandad". Aimee is fascinated by family lore.

Outside, Grandad had made a Christmas wreath at a Blore Heath "Crafternoon" and lays it on Bob and Eleanor's graveyard stone. They would have thrilled to see the church filled with young people, and enthusiastically singing Christmas songs. Well done to all for this super Christmas-in-church celebration.

21: Seeds - and a soft-play area

It is a Sunday afternoon in November. Grandad and Grandma have been out for a bit of lunch at the Hungersheath tearooms. The kettle is on but the sun is shining and the garden beckons. The phone rings. A small voice on the other end of the line wonders if Grandad is up for "sowing seeds". In next to no time, three keen gardeners are at the door, dressed up in outdoor gear. It's off to the polytunnel!

In next to no time, the team are busy finding seed packets from Grandad's motley collection of tins and boxes. Aimee (aged seven now) gets Grandad organised. She needs a seat, a work bench, seed compost, pots, labels, marker pen and crates to put the pots in. And down to business. Over the next hour plus, she has dozens of pots all neatly labelled. Daniel (three and a bit) wants to help. No problem - A. recruits him to fill pots and fetch and carry. He does brilliantly - "WELL-DONE D." from A. echoes around the polytunnel frequently.

Grandad relaxes happily unpodding his saved runner beans ready for next year.

Where is Callum, the keen reader will want to know. He has commandeered a defunct sheep trough. He thinks it will be a good planter. He and his brother (borrowed from duties with A.) fill it with good-quality potting compost that Grandad has been nurturing in a tractor-sized compost heap. Temporary turf war with A. over the use of plant labels averted, C. marks up sections for lettuce, strawberries, radishes and tomatoes and sows same.

A few weeks elapse... lettuce seeds are showing. Those doubters amongst you who might be saying' "Not much point sowing those seeds in November" might need to review their thinking - as Grandad has done. He has been proved wrong several times now, as seeds sown by C. appear as if by magic at different places in the garden.

Fast-forward a week. Again, lovely weather for time of year. Phone rings - does Grandad want to go for a walk down to pond? Gr. anticipates likely request for campfire and grub and fills bag with dry sticks and paper. Raids Grandma's secret cupboard for sweets. Whoops, don't forget matches Grandad...Down at pond, weather somehow made sticks and paper wet (how?). Very slow to get going. Hunt for dry-ish plant material. "My hands are freezing Da-da!" Callum off exploring. "Come and look Gr., I've found a playground". Gr. - ???

Willow-thicket (climbing frame!) has accumulated lots of dried leaves - soft to land on, like a (modern) playground area. Good thinking, C.!

Time to scoff the sweets...

22: A night in at the theatre

Dateline: Saturday 5.30 pm

Grandma wanted a night out. Perhaps a theatrical production? Online searching proved negative - nothing on at Drayton Festival Centre. Too far to go into Potteries or Telford. Disappointment imminent. But Grandad had to go across to neighbours to return DVD. Interesting invitation - "Grandad, would you and Grandma like to come to a show?" Grandad quite pleased: "As it happens, grand-daughters, that would be brilliant, because Grandma wanted to go out tonight to a theatre!"

Advance entrance tickets were priced at 20 pence each. Grandad hurried back to base to get dosh. Seats numbers one and two! Ace! What could be better? Grandma informed. No need to dress OTT, but be quick, performance starts 18.00.

Expectant grandparents installed in seats, tea supplied gratis. What will the show be? Who will be performers? Will there be music and dancing? Showbill:

> *SUPER DUDE* - A THEATRICAL
> PRESENTATION
> STARRING - Charlotte and Ellie
> *
> MUSIC - DANCE
> *
> Eat-your-hearts-out Morecambe and Wise fans!
> C. and E. present - a rapid-fire double act.
>
> SUPER DUDE AND FRIEND
> **
> Curtain calls

We just loved the music, dancing, jokes and - everything!

After many curtain calls, complete with cheers and much applause, everyone present declared what a fantastic theatrical experience was had by all...   When would be the next production? Put us on the mailing list!

With grateful thanks to C. and E. who did everything - scriptwriters, cast, directors, choreographers - not forgetting theatre hosts and caterers (Mum and Dad).

23: Noah's Ark

This month, Grandma is centre-stage.

Our local church is St Mary, Hales. We can see it from our farm. We were married there. Both our sons were baptised at Hales, and Rosie's parents are buried there. It used to be twinned with Ashley. There is a small, once-a-month Junior Church at Hales and Rosie and daughters-in-law go. Here is the story of what happened on the first Sunday in Lent...

The theme of the Sunday School was Noah's Ark. Three Hegarty grandchildren were there with Grandma and Mum, with a handful of other parents and children. A leader was telling the story of Noah's Ark when Rosie realises it is not entirely gripping the boys. Fortunately, Daniel (about three and a half now) had the foresight to take his tools with him (well a lad never knows does he when he might need chainsaw, hammers, spanners etc all in one's toolbox.). As attention waned and started to turn to said tool use, Grandma had inspiration. We can make a little "Noah's Ark" out of the kneelers! Three kneelers on the pew, two upright, one across = Noah's Ark.

Grandma did not anticipate that this idea would catch on as quickly as it did. The girls, not to be outdone by the lads, suddenly were creating a magnificently large Noah's ark with lots of kneelers. Talk about experiential learning and the use of a child's imagination! The church rapidly became replete with arks and the youngsters totally full on-message.

After juice for the boys and girls and tea and coffee for the adults, the event was pronounced a great success.

But wait a minute... D. had not had full use of his chain saw (anxious readers please see footnote). He was espied attacking a pew with same. Photograph duly taken for posterity (sadly not available to author at time of writing).

Hopefully, Hales Church regulars will not notice (or will not mind!) all the kneelers in different places next Sunday. But it was all in a good cause - think of all those animals saved! And, pew, miraculously, undamaged....

FOOTNOTE - you didn't think it was a real chainsaw, did you?

24: Manners, Grandad!

We adults just have to watch our p's and q's, don't we?

Daniel (aged coming up to 4) and Grandad (coming up to 60, nose growing longer) are sharing an art session. Now Grandad is not a confident dauber. No. But he is happy to sit and splosh some marks on canvas to support the upcoming van Goghs etc.

So there we are with an art project from Trago Mills (Falmouth— have you not discovered the delights of Trago Mills yet? You are missing out!) comprising a small canvas with a picture to colour in and 6 paints in tiny pots (plus brush). The careful side of Grandad likes the fact that this was LESS THAN A POUND. (Grandad buys a ruck of them when he and Grandma go to Falmouth to visit Cousin-Betty-from-Cornwall.)

Anyhow, of course, you have to keep your brushes clean. So Grandad sets up the painting table with pots of water, kitchen roll, etc. Of course, the water soon turns to a muddy brown colour and needs replenishing. Getting bored with always changing the water, Grandad goes off to the kitchen sink to clean the brushes.

Now it so happens that Grandma is washing up. Grandad just leans across and dabbles the brushes in a convenient pot of water.

Voice from behind: "Grandad, you must say 'Excuse me'."

Whoops, sorry D.

Fast forward a few days. Teatime around the kitchen table at D's place, Mum is deep in conversation with Aunty B. and Grandma. D. wants something (a drink I think but memory grows dim on details).

"Mummy, please can I have …."

Grandad (getting his own back?): "D. you must say 'Excuse me.'"

D: "Excuse me, mummy". But mummy is deep in conversation….

D: (as an aside to himself) "She cannot hear me."

(Grandad is impressed by this—psychologist in him thinks, great example of "theory of mind" [=awareness of what someone else is thinking].

D: (shouting loudly): "EXCUSE ME MUMMY PLEASE CAN I HAVE?."

… That worked! ….

25: Veg Box

"Can I help you Grandad?"

Ellie (granddaughter, now 8) appears on the allotment kitted out for outdoor working. It is evening time, the end of the first, glorious sunny day for what seems like weeks.

"Of course, E, what would you like to help with?" [Experience shows that it is best to let one's volunteers choose tasks they actually want to do.]

E. wants to pick something. Gr. explains that being Spring, there are only winter vegetables, not fruit. But no matter, how about if we put together a "veg box" that she can take into Mummy and Daddy? Quick-as-a-flash, E. says, "Can we sell it?"

Gr. is impressed by this entrepreneurial thinking and suggests that Mummy might indeed want to purchase fresh, organic vegetables straight from the garden. A quick trip to the recycling and re-use bay (yes, we have a whole area set aside at Blore Heath Farm for our three families to use) yields an appropriate box and we forage around the veg plot for produce.

We find: Jerusalem artichokes, Swiss chard, turnips, curly kale, cabbage tops, leeks. As some are a bit gritty, we need to turn on the hose to wash them down. High-power-jet-setting is great fun and we blast the dirt off the root veg, with gentle-spray option to rinse the greens.

Proudly the production team takes the veg box into the house. E. finds some sticky labels. "Vegetables" is duly written and affixed.

Time passes, Mum arrives home. She is very pleased to get an organic veg box, freshly picked and totally unexpected. Hasty, whispered Ellie request to Grandad, "How much [do I charge]"? Gr suggests £1.00...fortunately Mum pleased. Transaction completed. All parties chuffed.

The Hugo Meynell school headteacher can rest assured that his initiative to promote entrepreneurship at Hugo M. has, forgive the pun, yielded a rich harvest, at "Blore Heath Enterprises" at least.

26: Random veg

Committed readers of this column will recall that the grandchildren decided to have a gardening-fest late last year. Descending on the polytunnel, they wanted to have seeds and labels and sow them.

It was to no avail (actually Grandad did not even mention it) that November was no time really to be sowing lettuce and a myriad other bit of things left over in seed packets. But, this is Grandad's way of thinking, simply because he has never done that before!

So radish, lettuce, rocket, broad beans, peas and a host of left-over flower seeds were duly sown in the polytunnel and outside.

Similarly, Grandad only briefly mentioned to Callum and Daniel that it is best first to dig over the ground, then sow seeds in neat rows, and finally label them. Only briefly, because they were off with a "spade" each, as they call them (trowels) and digging a hole here, and a hole there, all over the place, and popping in seeds.

But lo and behold! Along comes April, and now (at the time of writing) early May, and what do we find? In the polytunnel I have lovely broad bean plants in one place, and little clumps of rocket in another! Outside, broad beans are popping up all over the place. And boy do they look healthy! Grandma and Grandad now are chuffed that they can go and get their own salad leaves without a trip to the shops.

P.S. Callum (aged 6 now-and going to Beaver Scouts in Ashley but that's for later "diaries") came home from the combined Hugo Meynell and Ashley Church pre-Easter service and saw Grandad's left-over willow twigs (remains of a Crafternoon, our then fortnightly craft sessions for older people at the farm). He wanted Grandad to cut one of the twigs in half—duly done. With some string lying around he then tied the two twig-halves in the form of a cross. "You should hang this up for Easter, Grandad." We looped the cross over a window catch and it hangs there still.

P.P.S. D. felt that his, now, 3-foot-high (not metric here at Blore Heath) solitary broad-bean plant with flowers now on needed SEEDS. So he placed, carefully, left-over broad bean seeds on the leaves.

C., moseying around minutes later, found same and excitedly announced that the plant had produced seeds.

27: Look, Grandad!

Daniel arrives home from Hugo-Meynell. He looks smart in his school uniform. Grandad cannot get used to this. He seems too young to go to school. But wait a moment - what has he taken with him to school today? Surely not, yes, out comes his chainsaw and ear- protectors. Grandad is reassured. What a progressive school to allow youngsters to take their work tools in. Well done, Headteacher and team. (D. goes half-days, b.t.w, just for the record.)   D. is ready for a bit of action, but he has to go in and get changed into his work clothes ... [short while later] ...D. appears, dressed in wellies and suitable gardening clothes. Grandad certainly needs some help as there are all the veggie and flower plots to weed. Trowels and spades and hoes and seed packets and fertiliser later - let battle commence…

Grandad gets absorbed, firkling out little weeds. Then:
"Grandad…?" …   "Yes, D.?"

D. wants to know if he can go into the shed. Grandad treks off to shed with D., unlocks it and D. extracts his preferred tool. Gr. returns to concentrate on weeding-out of all the lovely wildflowers that have somehow, by magic, appeared in the flower bed since last week. Now we are getting somewhere with the task-in-hand…...Then:
"Grandad? … …   "Yes, D.?"

D. is keen to sow some of the seeds he has just found in a packet in the polytunnel. Gr. toddles off to find another packet to decant some of them into. D. soon sprinkles the seeds on the flower bed. Great - soon we will have some annuals! Grandad returns to focussed extermination of all those pesky nettles that have somehow sprung up since 5 minutes ago when he last looked... Then:
"Look, Grandad…." Grandad is a bit pre-occupied now,

….

"Yes, D.?"
"Look, Grandad…" ("Yes, D.?") …
"Look, Grandad…" ("Yes, D.?")
"Look, Grandad…?"
But D. has had enough of Grandad's inattention and so Grandad, kneeling down, suddenly finds two small hands grabbing his head and turning it forcibly around and down…

"LOOK - GRANDAD".   That worked!

28: The wheel turns …

Grandad, aeons ago, when dinosaurs roamed Blore Heath, took Number 1 son to Cubs at Hugo Meynell. The then Akela announced that there would be a "parents meeting", a now-ominous phrase, the following Monday. Dutifully, many dads and mums turned up and sat on tiny chairs in classroom one. "I am giving up Cubs and so if you want it to continue someone will have to take over." On the way home in the car, brother-in-law Ian says: "You be Akela and I will help." And so it came to pass…. Gr. became Akela, then Group Scout Leader. Oh, how suggestible can one be!

Fast forward 30-ish years. Beavers (6–8-year-olds, pre-Cubs) starts up again, after years of a "no-leader situation". But soon, a "parents meeting" is announced. Ha-ha says Grandad, I know what that means. Gr. thought there was NO DANGER of being dragooned into being a LEADER again, as he was WELL OVER what used to be the COMPULSORY RETIREMENT AGE. Imagine his feeling of, er, amazement (not exactly the right word), then, when Grandad was informed that he could once again become a leader, the Scout Association having abolished the compulsory retirement age. Several forms later…… What was that about a wheel?

Since then, Grandad has been taking Callum to Beavers on Thursdays at Hugo Meynell. We enjoy the little trip in the car there and back with friendly chat and fun. Grandad has a bit of *déjà vu*, as he (see above) imagined he had retired from Scout leadership, but that's OK and Grandad had never thrown away his be-badged scout shirt and 1st Ashley Air Scout neckerchief with its unique RAF-affiliated squadron badge. And his woggles, some from his own cub and scout days in 23rd Manchester Birch-in-Rusholme Scout Group [it's still active, Google says and meets only a woggle-throw from the original scout hut, with its many happy memories].

C. is good company but of course Grandad has to watch his p's and q's now C is 6-going-on-7. Admittedly he (Gr.) does not necessarily tidy up his car daily. Books, church newsletters, till slips and the other stuff one puts on the passenger seat somehow assume a life of their own and wander around the car. C. gets in to go to Beavers one evening and says, rather parent-ly I thought, "Grandad, your car's in a bit of a mess." When I stuck my head out of the car and relayed this piece of advice to his mother as precocious - if correct (out of the mouths of babes and sucklings etc), C. retorted, "Well it is!" "It is, Grandad, it is!"

I'm definitely going to tidy up the car for next Beavers' night.

29: Dinosaur golf

A well-known local garden centre has spent probably a very tidy sum installing dinosaurs. They are quite lifelike (??!!) and move a bit (I think the word is animatronic) and dinosaur-like (??!!) noises come out of loudspeakers. So it's a whole new experience for Ashleyites. Anyhow, it seemed a perfect opportunity for a Grandad and Grandma outing - with the grandchildren naturally!

Dinosaur golf is crazy golf, which many grandparents will remember from family holidays in the 50s/60s, when there was not much else to do in the rare intervals of dry weather on the annual seaside holiday. You picked up your putting stick and golf ball and went round the windmills and other obstacles trying to get your ball down the hole. The *cognoscenti* remembered not to putt their ball down the last hole, because it invariably ended up in the kiosk; if you avoided this hazard you could go round again.

Ashley grandparents! You need not be disappointed! Dinosaur golf is the never-to-be-forgotten re-lived experience. Never mind that French guy and his madeleines, you can "*recherche les temps perdus*" at that well-known local nursery and "dinosaur park"! The kiosk is there, you still get the putting stick and ball (but, and this is progress, different colours for each player) and a score-card. And (and this is a clincher for the *recherche* experience) the last hole SENDS THE BALL INTO THE KIOSK!!!

Grandad, against his expectations, really enjoyed the dinosaur golf experience. It was great to see Daniel (just had his fourth birthday) using his initiative to "sweep" the ball into the holes, Callum (nearly 7) giving them a good bash, and Aimee (8) keen on keeping the score card up to date. Grandma (49 -?), true to earlier form (another story) was a bit heavy-handed with the old golf swing and, thinking she was at the Open, knocked her ball quite off-piste from time to time.

All in all, a fun experience. Grandad was just a tiny bit disappointed that the dinosaurs did not "do" more (too much *Jurassic Park*...?) but, hey, what do you expect from a round of mini-golf?

Next month - Grandad goes knee-trembling sky-walking at same venue.

30: Sky walking

Sometimes you just don't know what you are letting yourself in for. Flushed with the success of actually completing a round of dinosaur crazy golf (see last episode), Grandad was in a magnanimous mood. Next door to Dino Crazy Golf at the local well-known garden centre and multiple was the SKY TRAIL. The g/children were keen to go on it - OK!

Now Grandad did not actually read the advertising blurb before going with Aimee (8 years), Callum (7), Daniel (4) and Mrs Grandad. But if he had, he might well have had second thoughts. To quote the website: "Next to the Jurassic Golf you can find now our brand new "Sky Trail" High Rope Course. With 19 challenging obstacles to manoeuvre in height of nearly 15 feet, this definitely will be thrilling adventure for all the brave ones (5+)". "5+" - I mean, no worries, how difficult can something for over-fives be? (Quite difficult, frankly terrifying is the answer.)

D. was too young/small to be allowed on. His older brother and sister were old enough BUT HAD TO HAVE AN ADULT ACCOMPANYING. Yikes, thought Grandad who does not like fairground rides (not even the under-fives teacups ride on Llandudno pier), Grandma can go. But Grandma had shoes with heels - good excuse thought Grandad. Nothing for it when you gotta go. Having paid the not inconsiderable fee for the three of us, we processed through the portal. Very pleasant young men then proceeded to fit serious, and I mean serious, safety harnesses to each of us. A tug here and a buckle there - and then a strap thingy with a pulley on the top to slot into an overhead track. What is this, thought Grandad. So with our overhead strappy things above us, we started to climb up to the Sky Trail.

Keen to watch out for possible danger, Grandad let C. go first across Obstacle 1. A steel girder. C. did very well to get across it, then A. and then Grandad. WELL DONE, GRANDCHILDREN! (WELL DONE, GRANDAD!!). Knees shaking, you perch on a tiny platform, a crow's-nest affair, whilst recovering nerve for the next obstacle - your actual Peruvian rope bridge. We managed it, phew, but A., (praise the angels), had had enough.   The way down was quickly found. One of the nice young men (Polish, I asked him) said had Grandad enjoyed himself. "Errr, I'll have to think about that", said Grandad. Perhaps if I had had a bit longer on Sky Trail, I mean I had to come off early, thinking of the children.

I don't think I saw an upper age limit on the board outside. It seems you can go on, however old you are, as long as you are above a certain height. But probably best to take grandchildren with you - just in case you need a reason to cut your sky-walking short. And then you could go round the Dino Golf again.

31. Ding dong

Grandma and Grandad are so lucky to be living in close proximity to our grandchildren. We only have to look out of our bedroom window whilst drinking our morning cuppa to see them going off to school. Even Daniel (only just four) has now joined the long march to educational achievement as he starts at Hugo Meynell full time this term. But life is not all school! Then it's playtime!

We have one of those clever doorbells that doesn't have any wires. Press the bellpush and magically it rings some distance away - ding dong ding dong (your nose is this long, sshh don't tell the children bad habits...). Grandma can hear it better than Grandad who probably went to too many rock concerts at Uni. "There's somebody at the door." Often, that somebody is one of the grandchildren, but not D. - he is too small to reach the bell, but not to be outdone, he knocks on the door or the little pane of glass next to it.

The other week, Grandad goes to the door to discover whether it is someone telling him he has won the million pound Lottery prize (unlikely, we don't buy tickets) but in fact it is Ellie and Charlotte. Grandad greets them warmly – "Hey, great to see you ...err, how can we help." On this occasion they clearly knew why they had come even if Gr. did not. (This is not unusual, because there are ongoing plots to arrange things that Gr. has not been told about.) It seemed that a pact had been made for us to "mind" them for an hour or so whilst parents went to school meeting.

Grandad is usually prepared for pre-teenage-girl-sitting ("babysitting" no longer appropriate) and has a secret drawer with entertainment "stuff" in it. But as he did not know (or had forgotten etc - see above) he was caught on the hop. Grandma suggested they might watch TV but that somehow did not seem to cut the mustard - we had to do better than that. What can you entertain increasingly sophisticated pre-teen girls with? Go on readers - suggest something - quickly!! Fortunately, an idea emerged from the depths - hide and seek. We had Cousin-Betty-from-Cornwall with us so she soon got into the action. But, whereas 6 years ago, we could easily hide from the girls, now it was not so easy. A few hide-and-seeks later, the novelty was wearing off.

Drastic action required! Grandad turned himself into a zombie, only needing to touch a pre-teen to turn them also into the un-dead. Although Gr. had not reckoned on unleashed energy and had to fight for his life (death? as it were) with pre-teen-vampires wanting to kill him, and pull out his hair, and his heart.

Hey what's that? Ding dong ding dong - Mum and Dad are back. Phew, that's a relief.

32: Birthday party

Callum had a birthday this week. Confidentiality forbids me from ratting on how old he is but suffice it to say that he is not six any longer.

It has truly been a privilege to share in his getting older. Readers of the past episodes will have their own memories of our happy times together - "laddering" for example, when C decided it was imperative to take a ladder from the workshop and prop it up on all sorts of convenient structures, just to find out what it was like to climb up and have a look-see. Or times when C wanted to "go to the workshop and make a robot". And then there were the creations (still there) when C. climbed ladders and installed door handles high up on the barn beams.

Anyway, now we are older, and more adult pastimes rule. Such as "Minecraft". Minecraft is a comparatively new computer game...well, game is a tad misdemeaning for what is a really extremely sophisticated computer application. "Minecraft is a game about placing blocks to build anything you can imagine." This is what the Internet tells Grandad about it. For instance, so Internet says, at night monsters come out, and you have to make sure to build a shelter before that happens. Grandad, of course, is not speaking from personal experience here. But it sounds great.

C.'s family birthday party (there is usually one for the oldies and another one for the youngies now at each birthday) last week was superfabulous with a host of cousins and their respective families attending. There was great food and refreshments and then oldies went off to chat whilst youngies clustered around screens. Screens! You cannot get away from them now. There are mobile phone screens demanding service, and computer screens beckoning with the delights of the aforesaid Minecraft and more. Grandad's university students can walk up and down stairs whilst worshipping their screens without mishap...wow!

Avids of this series will want to know about the granddaughters. I cannot tell of what the granddaughters were doing - secrets not revealed to Grandad for this episode, but still involving screens. Feminine things, no doubt. But Daniel, on safer ground for Grandad, was immersed in "Farm Manager". This is just the job for budding farmers! Apparently, you get so much farm equipment and land etc and then you have to run your farm (virtually of course) and cope with the various hazards. It's engrossing for a four-year-old.

Thankfully, after a while D. can be seen outside on his tractor, loading gravel and tipping it in little piles on the patio....... You can't beat real life, can you?

33: Cake-a-thon

Our grandchildren are growing up - of course! We have loved so much their foibles and idiosyncrasies before they started school but now the varied pressures of modern life have started to have their inevitable impact. But, there are little islands of childhood still to explore! One of those islands is the weekly Beaver-scout meeting. Grandad has, as avids of this column will know, succumbed to what felt like destiny and assumed once more the mantle of a Scout leader, by becoming Beaver Scout Leader (or "Doc" as the Beavers and Beaver parents know him!).

Doc. is thankfully not building a lone log-dam, however. He has super help from other leaders, parents, and even teenaged youngsters, whom we call Junior Assistants. At the moment we have two Charlottes, Ruby, Tom and Mea, who are the older siblings of Beavers - all of them of older Cub Scout or Scout age and who contribute wonderfully to the Beaver meetings.

The last meeting of the Autumn term this year was devoted to a wonderfully topical evening - CAKE A THON - envisioned and organised by the Scout section leaders. Open to all the "sections" (Beavers, Cubs, Scouts and Explorers). The idea was to bring cakes which would be judged - just like TV's The Great British Bake Off!

Well, what a super evening! The cakes were unbelievable. Not just any old cakes but super-decorated, immaculately constructed culinary edifices that even Mary Berry would have been impressed by. And there were games and a raffle.

Grandad went with Callum, as usual for Beaver meetings along with Mum and younger brother Daniel. D. (aged 4 now) was a bit unsure with all the Beavers, Cubs, Scouts, leaders and parents there, so Grandad took him round to see what was what.   What's that? Santa has come?? Off we go to get first in the queue for the grotto. In goes D., Grandad has to wait. .... What are they doing in there? D. has certainly had his money's worth! Santa obviously was having a big chat with D. Out he came with a present, all nicely wrapped. What was it? Santa obviously knew just exactly what D. wanted - lots of chocolate.

Soon all was scoffed and Grandad's final role for the evening was clear. What was that? Well, nicely-brought-up youngsters know they mustn't throw wastepaper on the ground. So what do they do with it?   Give it to Grandad - of course.

34: Hide and Seek

It doesn't seem all that long ago when grand-daughter Charlotte (now 10) was quite little and loved playing Hide and Seek with Grandad. For a young pre-schooler, Hide and Seek can be a difficult game to learn. The most fun thing about it at that age is being caught, so some of the niceties of the game seem less important and harder to grasp. For example, knowing where to hide. And, not choosing the same place to hide each time. Or waiting until "Coming, ready or not" marks the start of the search. And, of course, keeping quiet whilst someone is looking for you. We played it time and time again, and there was always some little nook or cranny to hide behind, even in the small house they were renting then.

The other day, history was repeating itself with grandson Daniel, now 4 and a bit or so. Callum (7) and younger brother D. came to be "minded" and C. wanted to play hide and seek. Now he, being older, is a sophisticated hider and seeker, but D. was a bit unsure, so Grandad and he hid and sought together. Our house has lots of good hiding places for the younger player, but not so much for the more sophisticated. Would it be exciting enough??

Gr. and D. started off by hiding somewhere pretty cunning, but C. soon found us. C's turn. Grandad, confident it would be a cinch to find the seven-year-old, boldy set off with D. in tow on a sophisticated search-and-locate mission at one end of the house. Grandad wasn't wearing his glasses so walked past C. once (crouching under a desk). Fortunately, D's sharp young eyes came to the rescue and his brother was duly unearthed from his hidey-hole.

Grandad and D had no more success with their second hiding place, clever as it was (Grandad thought). C.'s turn again. "1, 2, 3…...20. Coming ready or not." Off we set again on our search. To no avail. First sweep of the area - negative. No C. Second sweep, this time making sure all the likely places were investigated. Negative. Had C. slipped out of the house and gone to his own domicile (next door)? No, unlikely. Abducted by aliens? Who knows? So where on earth was he……?

Ding dong ding dong. Yikes!! There's mum at the door and we have lost one of her sons - abducted by aliens? Just starting to confess that we actually could not find him; when …

"Here I am", a voice rings out. "Where were you hiding?" Grandad wants to know.

"Behind the Christmas tree!"

We looked but never saw. You won, C!!

35. How to play Zombies

It's half-term. Grandad and Grandma are to host Ch. (10) and E. (8) whilst parents are earning pennies. What to do with increasingly sophisticated young ladies?

The morning is pretty well planned-out: ice skating lessons at Telford Ice Rink. Grandma knows how to get to Telford - but where is the ice rink exactly? Grandma's new car has a satnav. Grandad punches in the postcode. Will it tell us how to get there? Grandad firkles in the glovebox (are they still called that?) for the Manual. Cannot miss it - about 4 inches thick, or whatever that is in cm. "Search by postcode" - yes, doing that. "Press the GO button to get the map". Errr - what GO button?? After several repeats of exactly the same process we are in Telford and Grandad has still not got to GO. Voice from rear - "Turn here Grandma and then you will see it." Hey ho.

They had a good time. Now what to do? Home for a drink. Grandad gets out a "stone painting kit" he bought to occupy grandchildren. Perfect … well, so he thought. Not interested really. What then? "Can we play that game Grandad where you pretend to be a zombie?" On the basis that other readers of this column would like to play this game, here's how to play it……

HOW TO PLAY "ZOMBIES"

You will need: A reasonably large bungalow/house/mansion/palace where players can run around screaming whilst trying (not) to be caught by the Zombie. A Grandad. No neighbours. Pre-teen children (possibly girls, boys seem too intent on fighting Zombie). A tolerant Grandma with good excuse to end game in case of Grandad exhaustion.

Before playing: It is essential to warm up. This takes about 15 minutes, possibly longer with a bit of luck. Players ask the Grandad if he will play Zombies. Initially he pretends he has not heard (sometimes he hasn't). Request is repeated, louder. The Gr. grunts. This might mean yes, no or incipient zombie-ism. Then a brew must be started, and tea drunk. Players ask the Gr. repeatedly have you finished tea yet etc etc - grunt grunt. All of a sudden, the Grandad turns into a ZOMBIE.

Playing: The Gr. walks around like something out of Curse of the Mummy's Tomb, or Night of the Walking Dead (Grandad has not seen any other films as he does not like horror films, but those were clearly stupid, so not very horrific, but he only watched a bit of them anyway). Players run away screaming until allowing themselves to be caught and carried off to be dumped in a grave. (Sofa, then covered with cushions.) Hiding places like locking themselves in the toilet is permissible. Zombie scratches at door, makes frightening noises etc etc

Close of play: The game is finished when players are fed up (can take a long time), or the Gr. is worn out, children's parents arrive, or Grandma reminds Gr. he should not get carried away and over-exerted and possibly then become a candidate for zombie-hood.

36: Card Games

We like games here at the Blore Heath homestead. Last time, I explained how to play "Zombies" - and granddaughter Charlotte thought my Diary of a Grandad entry last month about this was very funny. Thanks, Ch.! Of course, I copy her in now to my diary entries as well as her mum to make sure she is happy with stuff about her and her sister and cousins being published.

But we don't just play Zombies! No, we have really intelligent games as well. Like SNAP. Now come on readers, when did you last enjoy a game of Snap? Possibly you are into Whist? Or, for the very sophisticated, Bridge. Me, I like Solo Whist. If I had plenty of time and space, I would go into raptures about Solo Whist and how about one time I had an *Abondance declaré* (lay-down your hand after the first trick to get all 13 tricks, no trumps). I was so chuffed I can still remember! Anyhow I digress.

The other night we were tweeny-sitting (soon it will be grandad and grandma-sitting I think), so what shall we play? (It being too late to play Zombies, thus over-excited Grandad.) SNAP seemed to be the consensus.) (Now, it has to be said that Grandma can be rather competitive. Yes. Grandma cannot bear to lose at Musical Chairs. So, readers, be warned. Do not play Musical Chairs with Grandma. No. Anyhow, we have not taught grandchildren to play that yet. Adult games to come later.)

Grandad likes to win at SNAP. He does this by being very, very focussed on the cards and making sure his hands are super close to the cards being put down (reaction time is a mathematical function of "movement time" + "decision time", as his psychological training has taught him). In other words, you have to realise that the two cards just placed are the same AND slam your hands down on the cards as quickly as possible. Given that incipient brain-rot militates against fast decision time, at least you can minimise the distance your hands have to travel.

Ch. and E. will tell you that Grandad wins partly because he shouts SNAP so LOUDLY that everyone else suffers from shock. Of course, no self-respecting Grandad could admit to that. Anyway, the granddaughters have their own strategies - like thinking and moving a lot quicker. Hey ho. So they tend to win on balance.

Drat. Anyone for ZOMBIES?

37: News

The months roll by and all our lovely grandchildren are finding new things to do. Charlotte enjoys swimming and can do what Grandad never managed—those somersault turns when you come to the end of the swimming bath. She can do them when swimming front and back crawl. Wow. Grandad was really into swimming at her age and went with friend Peter as often as possible to "High St Baths" in Manchester. They are no more but an action group won a TV appeal to save them from ruin.

Ellie and Aimee are into dancing and are very fortunate to have their dancing school (Oak Tree Dance Studio, with Miss Penny) literally on their doorstep. Grandad did a bit himself way back, rising to dizzy heights of President of the Ballroom Dancing Society (colloquially, rudely, Ball Soc) at Nottingham University [actually this was because no-one else would do it]. That was a lot of fun: Beginners class from 6 pm, then half-hour down in the bar before Improvers at 8. The second class always seemed to go better than the first, I don't know why.

Callum helps Grandad by going with him to Beavers and carrying all the boxes of stuff, most importantly the sponge footballs which the Beavers absolutely love booting around the hall. Ch. also helps at Beavers by the way.

The youngest, Daniel, is into all sorts of things but especially helping Gr. in the garden and polytunnel. He makes up his own projects, especially digging ones, and sometimes tidies up afterwards.

But what about Grandad? Well, Gr. very much enjoyed helping brother Geoff crash, I mean build and fly, his model planes. I could tell you all sorts of stories about those projects. Normally they did not fly very well. One of them that we launched in Birch Park flew up and up and got stuck in a tree. It could be still there because there was no way we could get it down. We realised early on you had to expect them to come to a sticky end.

Anyhow, becoming Beaver leader of Ashley AIR scouts therefore has been a great excuse, I mean reason, to try and recreate those happy times. On the farm and at Beavers we've made paper aeroplanes and had great fun chucking them around. Some even fly quite well. Grandad's always looking out for new model aircraft to try and the latest is a radio-controlled one made out of foam. It has two propellers behind the wings powered by little motors. (That's good because they don't break when it nose-dives to the ground.) You charge the tiny batteries up, set the props whirring, throw it into the air and it flies amazingly well, but round in circles before diving to the ground. C. and I had great fun with this in our farm loft, ducking as it whirled around our heads, narrowly missing. Lucky it was made of foam.

38: Art sale

"ART SALE". Notices were everywhere. Who could resist? In I went, but it was too early. "We are not open yet. Please come back later."

"Later" duly arrived and Gr. went across the yard to see if the art sale had commenced. It was certainly a scene of industry. All the grandchildren were busy creating products for sale. There were drawings, buttons made into earrings, stones being painted, stone-painting have-a-go ("30p Grandad"). Wow, what a cornucopia of shopping delight. Grandad was so tempted by everything that he had to go into the house and raid the pot-containing-loose-change.

What to choose 'though? Well, he obviously had to have a little bit of everything. A button-made-into-an-earring was a must as a present for Mrs Grandad. A couple of paintings, yes. But what really caught G's eye was the painted stones. Gr. likes painted stones! Actually, he first came across the idea at a Croxton church event for youngsters. Gr. is not really an artist, but he loved painting patterns on pebbles. We have a lot of pebbles at Blore Heath—they are lying there in the fields just waiting to be picked up. Gr has used that activity a lot. Even Keele University "ecotherapy" students have painted pebbles. It blew the mind of one student. Wow, he said, that is so off the wall, Dr H. People on open days at Green Age barn have painted pebbles. Counsellors at training days have painted them. Wow, how versatile is that activity! But best of all, we have painted them here at Blore Heath with the g/children, especially Callum. So I just had to have one of his painted pebbles at the Art Sale. It's on my desk now.

Time goes on...It's Saturday afternoon and respective parents are away somewhere. E. and A. ring the bell —"Ding Dong".

"Can we come in please?"   "Of course! What do you want to do?"

"Grandad, have you got Swan Lake?"

Of course! Spotify has most things [other streaming websites are available etc....]. Just the job, a bit of Tchaikovsky! Then we get a super display of ballet moves *à la* Swan Lake.

"Grandad, have you got .... *Stitches*?"

Grandad is in unknown territory here, having spent the afternoon swotting up the songs for the May Community Choir Concert.

Stitches? With the help of that music-streaming website Gr. came up trumps. But I don't think Peter will want the community choir to sing it.

Why not? Check it out, and you'll see!

39: Diary of a Zombie

Grandad is no more. He has been turned into a ZOMBIE. Avids of this series will no doubt recall that a BIG HIT with the grand-daughters and grand-sons is a home-grown game called ZOMBIES. It all started with Grandad acting the fool and pretending to be one of the actors from "Night of the Living Dead" B-movie from aeons ago. Not that Grandad actually watched it cos it was too scary; he just saw the trailer and got the idea of how to walk like an undead person. For some obscure reason the grand-children loved this "game", and a replay is often requested, as for example the other day...

.... Ellie (now about 10, possibly, G/dad cannot tell) was over at ours for an hour or so whilst parents were off doing important things. Grandad was on the allotment when E. appeared. "Can I help you Grandad?". Now I have to say that E. is not what you would call a get-your-hands-dirty kind of young lady. I have learned over the years of having young people "help" me in the garden that the best plan is to find something that they WANT to do, not what you need doing. So, bit of a cross-examination:

"Would you like to sow some seeds?"

"Not really Grandad. [NRG]" ..."

"What about weeding?" NRG.... ....

"I know, let's do a flower arrangement."

Actually that appealed and we whiled away 15 minutes doing that.

"What about pressing some flowers in your flower press?"

"Well that takes a long time, Grandad."

Grandad thought it time to defect to the house where Grandma doubtless had fascinating young-lady-type-of-things to do. But not to be! Grandma's idea to make a felt puppet did not really appeal...

"Grandad???" (Hear cajoling, hesitant and plaintive voice.)

"Yes, E.?"

"Can we play Zombies?" [Ah so that was what it was all about.......!]

At this point, grandson Daniel (nearly 5) comes on the scene and decides he would like to play too. There are different play-tastes of course. E. liked being chased and captured and taken to the Zombie cave (=settee) and covered in heavy rocks (=cushions). (Grandma is fortunately quite tolerant about furnishings being thus elevated to fantasy games props.) D. on the other hand grabbed the nearest available weapons and attacked the Zombie ferociously. Cushions, bits of wood, a plastic sword, in fact anything, were used in the onslaught. "That hurt actually, D." did not cut much ice—the Zombie was to be defeated.   Thankfully you cannot kill a zombie...

40: Afternoon tea

Knock knock. Ding dong ding dong, your nose is this long....

"Someone at the door, Rosie!" (If Rosie answers phone or sees visitor *etc* it saves Grandad half-hearing it all then having to tell Rosie everything that has just transpired but getting bits wrong.)

It's Daniel (5 now, just had birthday) with a verbal invitation. He is getting really good at delivering messages. "Afternoon tea is at 2 o'clock or 3 o'clock." "Which one, D?" ...... He runs off to check. 3 confirmed. "Where, D?" He disappears again. "You will get an invitation later."

(Later) Ding dong etc. Small faces peering through the glass by the side of the door. Two handmade invitations duly presented. "You are invited to afternoon tea at 3pm in the yard." Grandad goes off to appointments with strict instructions to be back for tea. Grandad is a tad late, tho', and tea is already being served.

Imagine the scene, dear reader. Two big tables have been put end to end in our "yard" (communal space in front of our three houses) and they are set out with crockery and cutlery and teacups and saucers. The five g/children are dressed up as waiters with aprons, the girls in white blouses and dark skirts. On the table we have plates of sandwiches, chocolate cakes, shortbread, marshmallows with melted chocolate to dip into, scones with jam. Starters are served fruit threaded onto skewers. Tea is poured. Caroline has been up since 7am she tells us supervising the baking, which all g/children have helped with. D. was *chef-de-shortbread*. It was super-yummy.

Dr. and Mrs Grandad, with their recent cruise holidays fresh in mind, are connoisseurs of afternoon tea. In fact, it is not an exaggeration to say that we went halfway round the world to have afternoon tea at Raffles in Singapore. And we paid a princely extra sum to be served afternoon tea on the observation lounge on our cruise ship. I have to tell you 'though, that these were pale imitations of the wonderful afternoon tea in the Blore Heath yard. Grandad especially liked the shortbread. Well done, D!

And we did not get, at those exotic locations, the treat that followed tea. Aimee and Ellie gave a musical performance of songs from *Sound of Music*, followed by a solo performance from E. of a modern pop song. After plenty of thanks and claps the children disappeared to do their own thing.

Eat your heart out, Raffles!

41: Patriarch takes part in a holiday club

It's been quite a summer holiday, G/dad-wise. Summer is a difficult time for working mums and dads and so grandparents can play an important part in keeping the children occupied. We've been so lucky this year in Ashley because we have had no less than TWO WEEKS of church "holiday clubs".

Week number one was the PYRAMID ROCK holiday club. Organised by the Benefice Young People's Team, with the help of the Rev and Mrs Steve from Wetley Rocks, PYRAMID ROCK explored the story of Joseph and its biblical importance. What a fantastic week! Every morning, your editor and lots of helpers supported some 30 local youngsters to explore the Old Testament story of Jacob and Joseph.

The following week, rehearsals started for a production of Joseph and his Amazing Dreamcoat. No pressure, as they say, but it had to be learned in a week! Words, music, stage directions, costume changes - all had to be mastered by the cast, comprising Benefice youngsters and one oldie, your editor, playing the part of Jacob - patriarch, also shepherd (picture). Laughter allowed!

Grandad was chuffed to be taking E. and Ch. to both these events. Ellie loves dancing and singing, whilst Charlotte is interested in the production side of things.

Grandad is a bit sentimental about this. He remembers his Dad's ("Bob") older brother, Uncle Jack, who was really kind and generally child-focussed. Jack and Bob used to be very active in their church in Manchester - as was their father who used to go to church three times on Sunday and twice in the week. Whilst Dad played the piano, Jack would recite monologues and sing songs. Perhaps there is a "thespian gene" in our family?

You know, I bet there are very few places where youngsters could go to two whole weeks of holiday clubs such as we have had in Ashley.

42: Oil is your best friend

Our grandchildren are like trees. They are growing taller and are branching out with their interests and hobbies.

Charlotte Is now 10 and enjoys swimming. She can do all the strokes and is very fast. She even does those triathlon thingies where they swim, and cycle and run.

Ellie is a little bit younger and is into dancing and singing. She loves the musicals like Joseph, Cats and Annie. Wow! She liked being in our Ashley production of "Joseph" (see last entry.)

Aimee is a similar age to E. She dances too, and we get frequent impromptu song and dance performances.

Next in age is Callum, aged 7 and about to be leaving Beavers. He likes making things and brought in a super Meccano (yes, oldies, they still have it!) drag-racing car he made the other day.

Last in line, age-wise, is Daniel who is well into farming machinery. If G/dad steps out of line with putting his tractor in the wrong place he soon puts him right!

Whilst we are talking about D., I must tell you a little story. It happened the other week. Mrs G/dad was trying to shut a door into the utility room, and it would not just click shut. D. said, "You need some WD40, Grandma, oil is your best friend." Well, that really tickled us - "Where have you got that from, D?" D said it was one of his friends who told him Anyway, a bit later, D. and his family were going off on holiday and D. got himself a bit over-wrought. Sad to say, there were tears. (G/dad knew what he was feeling - sometimes, things get just a bit too much, especially when going on holiday.) Now, as it happened, Grandad had just bought some little plastic bottles of oil from the farmers' supermarket in Drayton. With a flash of genius, he gave one to D. and said "Oil is your best friend, D." That did the trick. Harmony reigned. He took the bottle with him on holiday and brought it back, thankfully unopened and so no mess in the luggage.

Top tip: Oil is your best friend.

43: Pont Aven

Readers of the Mag will remember that, *de temps en temps*, Cousin-Betty-from-Cornwall makes an appearance. Betty is Rosie's cousin who lives in Falmouth. She and husband Les used to keep a very popular chip shop in Falmouth and so she knows practically all the locals down there. When we go and stay we meet her friends and often play cards with them. A game called "Sequence" is very popular - have you come across it? It's easy but fun to play with friends.

Anyhow, in the course of our visits we have got to know Annie. Annie was born in France but met an English pilot and came to live in Falmouth. She still has a lovely French accent so it is easy to forget she has lived in UK for most of her life! (Be patient, I'm getting to the point of this tale.) Annie has a house that belongs to her family in a little village on the south coast of Brittany, near Pont-Aven. If you are arty at all that is a town well worth visiting. It has over 60 tiny art studios and a really splendid modern museum. Its main claim to fame is its association with Paul Gauguin who apparently was thrilled by the quality of the light. For a period of time around in the late 1880s he lived and painted there and attracted lots of artists to go and paint there.

En bref, as they say, our family has been to stay *chez* Annie *en France* several times now. Daniel was intrigued by the bits of French I was muttering and wanted to learn some basics. So, he got quite good at "*Ca va?*" and "*Merci*" and used them to good effect when they subsequently went over to stay, thanks to kind Annie. They came back with useful inside information about a really top-notch ice-cream parlour that, they said, we just HAD to visit the next time we went.

Unfortunately, when we ourselves went at half-term practically everywhere had shut up shop for winter. Except our favourite supermarket, thank goodness, which is a delight to explore and where we spend far too much buying chocs and biccies for presents back home. *A bientôt!*

44: Walnut football

Grandad is babysitting with Grandma whilst Ch. and E's parents are out for the evening. I think they have gone Chinese locally. Actually, "babysitting" is totally the wrong word for Charlotte and Ellie are what used to be called, "tweenies". That is, between childhood and teenage. Ch. Is ten now and E. is nine (Gr. thinks that's right ... their ages keep changing and it's hard to keep up.)

Grandad reminisces back to when Ch. was about 3 and E. still a baby. We would play hide-and-seek in the tiny house that they all lived in then. The key thing was to hide in almost the same place but not quite. There were not many places to hide. Gr. would squeeze into tiny doorways or behind curtains. But it was a lot of fun I can tell you!

Now the grandchildren are older and pretty sophisticated with their various e-gadgets. And you would not believe how advanced the practice papers are for SATS! Some of my uni students should do the English punctuation and the Maths for revision!! But the g/children still like to play "proper" games.   Tonight, we played card games first-off. SNAP! is a favourite - but Grandad had to be told not to shout very loudly as it scares the new puppy Lila. (She is like a little sheep, all covered in fluffy white hair and ever so tiny.) Then we played what used to be called Pelmanism, or more prosaically, "Pairs", Grandad was useless tonight and Ch. swept the board.

What shall we play now, Grandad? Inspiration came to Grandad when he remembered early evenings at home in Manchester. Dad would clear the kitchen table and knock in pins at either end to make goals. Shove Ha'penny! Or "Shuv'a'penny" as it sounded then. To be honest, Grandad never really got into it but his Dad enjoyed it! Memories of times in the RAF mess perhaps?

Gr. could not remember any rules so made them up - cross between billiards and football, using coins. We had the benefit of a smooth table. You don't need much tackle. Two walnuts blu-tacked at either end were goals (you don't have to use walnuts...hazlenuts would do, or almonds....). A 2p coin each as your player and a 5p for the ball. A ruler to try and score a goal by getting your player (2p) to knock the ball (5p) into the opposing goal. Eat your heart out Snooker on TV - this was fast and furious action.

Grandad was lucky and won 3-1, but I bet you Ch. and E. are secretly practising for the next tweeny-sitting session.

45: Back by popular demand

I am sorry that Diary of a Grandad has been absent for so long [six months]. Our lovely grandchildren have been growing up of course and they have so many other things to do than come to Grandad for trips to the pond – or to play "Zombies" (see previous episodes). So Grandad hasn't had much to write about. But today I had a deputation! Yes! Ellie and Aimee (now approaching their last year at Hugo) inquired, "Why are you not writing Diary of a Grandad, Grandad?" they wanted to know. They wanted it to re-appear.

Hoping to palm off a job on to them, Gr. suggested that they go off and write it themselves. But that did not seem to find favour. They were pretty bored, really, it being the end of the summer holidays. Dance workshops, sleep-overs, camping trips, swimming, summer films, holidays and so on had all taken their toll and they were yearning, so it seemed, for some good, old-fashioned Blore Heath Farm fun.

Truth to tell, Grandad, was not too keen on the first suggestion - "Can we play Zombies, Grandad?" It takes quite a bit of time for Grandad to build himself up to this energetic and, yes, quite involving game which, Grandad is proud to say, he invented. Yes! You cannot play it with just anyone - it is too epic! See diary entries no.35 and 39 for detailed instructions for you to play Zombies.

Frantically thinking on his feet, Grandad suggests a brand-new game – FIND THE MONEY! Doling out 10 coins, everyone has to take it in turns to hide the coins outside in the yard. This works surprisingly well and slowly quite a few of the Blore Heath inhabitants join in. A bit like "Hunt the Thimble", someone hides the coins and then everyone searches for them. When they are found (with a bit of help if necessary from the hider, as in "You are getting warm, hot, roasting..." etc.), it's someone else's turn. (Do you want to come and play? – just email!)

Soon, eldest granddaughter Charlotte Is leaving Hugo for secondary school whilst the other young ladies Ellie and Aimee will be thinking about that important transition soon. The boys, Charlotte (8) and Daniel (6) are busy with Minecraft and other video games that are a dark art to Grandad. But reassuringly, Callum still loves to go and play in the mud of the pond.

Maybe that's a good topic for another episode of Diary of a Grandad...

46: Stuck in the mud.

Our lovely grandchildren are back at school this month (I am writing this at the beginning of September). It is an ENORMOUS time especially for Charlotte who starts her secondary school - on her own, as it were. She leaves early in the morning to catch the bus to her school and arrives later than all the others at night. Ch. was really chuffed to be able to get into her secondary school (but she did work hard for months on extra homework) and wears her new uniform with pride. Still, it's hard for her to be an outsider, as it were, the others in our little community still being together and going to Hugo. What was lovely was that Aimee and Ellie made a banner for Ch., to welcome her home on her first day: WELCOME HOME CHARLOTTE.

Callum (8 now) has always had a penchant for the sensation of dirt and mud. On a recent trip to the farm pond he was entranced by the muddy area in the middle. "Don't get stuck in the mud!" said Grandad with his boring head on. What happened? Next thing, "I am stuck, Grandad". Hearing the voices of one's own parents in one's head, one thinks but does not say "I told you so". Elder son M. was on hand and duly went to rescue him. Have you ever tried rescuing someone stuck in the mud? No? So think about it for a moment.... the stuck person has ventured (in wellies) onto a dampish area (which was reasonably solid) and then into a muddier area which obviously (in hindsight) was not. The mud is glutinous and resists all efforts by the unfortunate en-mired person to extract their feet. The harder you try to push on one foot to pull the other out, the deeper that foot becomes. You are truly "in the mire". But then along comes an adult, who is heavier, has bigger wellies and - yes - you guessed it - there is a great possibility of that person also becoming well and truly stuck. (I know.) This is a case of "Don't panic Mr Mainwaring". You have to look around for a plank of wood to push to the bogged-down person for them either to push against or for the saviour to stand on and get some purchase. (It's entertaining to watch, by the way.) Duly extracted, and very muddy C. enjoyed it so much he went back in and did it again...ahem!

C. is now quite a bit older than when he and Gr. regularly went to the pond for adventures, and when, coming back, it was, "Can you carry me Grandad?" It was uphill all the way back and so Gr. would hoist a very muddy little chap onto his shoulders and was certainly out of breath when back at base. Now there is no way that could happen as he is just too big so it was great that he set off by himself for home, dripping wet and covered in mud like some swamp monster.

47: Halloween and more mud

Gr. is just off to a Halloween party at the neighbours'. Note the possessive plural - we are so lucky to have our five grandchildren living next door and opposite our house.

There is a knock at the door. Aimee has arrived with a beautifully party invite. Grandad is assured of a welcome as he has bought INDOOR FIREWORKS. And SPARKLERS. And little wind-up HALLOWEEN GHOSTIES. I will tell you about the party later on.

Yesterday was another adventure down at the Blore Heath pond. With the recent rains there is more water than there has been (see Diary 46). That is to say it is not simply mud, but mud with water over the top. Grandad was just settling down in the afternoon to writing this diary when a deputation arrived from over the yard (or patio if you want to be posh), to the effect could he come down to the pond. Eldest Granddaughter Charlotte was in the lead. She had just been to a friend's and had built a shelter out of branches and was keen to try out the design here. Gr. went armed with firelighting equipment, as there can be no proper expedition without a campfire. It reminds Grandad of his scouting days.

[Warning- reminiscence alert. I still cannot hardly believe that a requirement of the Scout First Class Badge, was that you went on an overnight hike with a friend to a destination you only found out about when you opened, on Scout's Honour, sealed instructions. You took tent and food etc with you and had to map-read to the 14 miles endpoint. There were no mobile phones, and nobody had any idea where you had to got to until you arrived, hopefully, home and then reported at the next weekly Scout meeting with your hike log completed. Does that, could that, happen now?? I went on a lot of these with fellow Scouts. Apart from getting very wet, blisters and nearly having the tent once trampled on by cows, nothing really untoward happened.]

C., now a veteran of Blore Heath ponding, soon stripped to the waist and set off into the pond. It was a beautifully warm day for the end of October and the pond area is quite a sun trap, so quite pleasant really. He decided to "surf", standing on a plank. Egged on by sister Aimee and cousin Charlotte he had a great time and did not even lose his balance. Meanwhile Gr. made a bit of a fire which at least made the subsequently soaked grandchildren think their clothes might dry out. After emptying welly boots of water, and wringing clothes out as much as possible, a squelchy trio trekked back over the fields to tea and warmth. Grandad hoped the respective washing machines would not break down by trying to cope with volumes of gritty mud... but the answer was to put them in the bin, he learned later.

48: Beggars

Where do they get it from? We might blame TV - or current affairs lessons at school? Yesterday and the day before we were plagued by immigrants/refugees begging at the door. Rat-a-tat-tat. We have a door knocker. The fancy wireless or infra-red or whatever fancy doorbell has given up the ghost. Our knocker is shaped as the head of William Wordsworth. A former graduate student (knowing of my love for Wordsworth's poetry) spotted it in an antique shop and thought that I could not do without it. Anyhow, upon opening the door - there are two little beggars. Further inspection of their bedaubed and made-up faces revealed - Aimee and Ellie!

Now it has been said that our granddaughters are very quiet at school. Of course, Grandad could not possibly subscribe to gossip. In the words of Francis Urquhart that wonderful TV series House of Cards, "You might say that, but I could not possibly comment." Well, if any of their teachers at Hugo are reading this, I can only say, come and stay with us for a while. They were very (and I mean, very) impressive beggars. Dressed for the part, with all the patter. (We know, we have seen them in the flesh in Romania.) And extremely persistent. Money (only a small amount), biscuits, drinks, threats, all failed to send them back home. They even suggested (because they were "homeless") that we leave the house so they could live here!

We've had a spate of birthdays. The latest is Charlotte now twelve years old. 12! (Can you believe it? We remember helping her to take her first baby steps!). The absolutest, bestest thing for Ch. Was the latest an i-phone. Grandad does not allow himself to have a "smart-phone". He will lose it. He has already lost 3 not-smart phones (thank goodness for the wonderful shop in Market Drayton that sells ones with actual buttons for £10). Cousin Callum. has a birthday coming up. He has asked for a massive pack of gel-pens. Gr. and Grandma understand that. Gr. is adding a pack of air-drying modelling clay, as C. loves getting his hands in dirty, sticky mud and stuff (see earlier diaries) for some more, old-fashioned play.

Ch. contributed a wonderful poem on the "Arctic" for the December issue of the Parish Magazine (see later in this book). When she sent it to me she had spelled "Arctic" as "Artic". No! Ch. and her dad and yours-truly are very proud of their spelling accuracy. What to do? Politely and as diplomatically as possible, in his role as editor, one suggested to Ch. that perhaps, she might wish to change the spelling to the more conventional, "Arctic". She was OK about that. Except ... the following night, she commented that Grandad was wearing his trying-to-be-trendy "Norwegian Explorer" fleece. Full of badges, one of them proudly sports a logo saying "Artic Exploration" [read that again!]. She pointed it out. *Touché*, Grandad!

49: Getting messy for church

One thing that has been bugging me is that I have not said much recently about our youngest grandchild - Daniel. So it's been great that in the past week, he and I have had the opportunity to do stuff together more than before. That opportunity arose, courtesy of "Messy Church".

Some of you will know what "Messy Church" is. The idea is that you lay on lots of craft activities suitable for youngsters of different ages and combine them with a worship opportunity. Children from Hugo have come *en masse* (in buses, during school time) at Christmas and Easter over the past year to the church where they have enjoyed a range of different activities laid on by church regulars. Grown-ups had a great time devising all kinds of different religious things such as angels and nativity scenes, or depictions of Easter (and I think the children have had a great time too!).

Well, a new initiative is to run these Messy Church events every month - to be exact, the last Saturday of each month, at the Hugo Meynell School. The first was last month when the theme was "Noah's Ark". Yours truly could not dream up a craft idea based on this so he volunteered, with Mrs Grandad, to be on the "catering team".

Now it has to be admitted that Grandad thought he would be on an easy wicket, just helping out a bit here and there with drying up the dishes or whatever. Imagine his excited surprise on arrival, to be told that, no, he (and Mrs G) WERE THE ENTIRETY OF THE CATERING TEAM. Wow! No matter, a Scout is always prepared! Grandad had come with all sorts of stuff ready for making beans and cheesy oatcakes, like for example his own microwave (non-digital thus easy to understand with ordinary knobs), tin opener (people always forget tin openers), etc etc. And... youngest grandson - D.

D. - what a hero. He said he wanted to come and help. Great. He was really keen and so helpful. There were lots of things for him to do, he already knowing his way around the school: doors to be held open, lights to switch on, chairs and tables to help move. He was ace at pouring beans from their cans into the slow cooker, and finding various utensils, jugs and so on in the kitchen area.

The event was deemed a great success, with lots of people coming, And D., tired but happy, is looking forward to Messy Church next month.

50. Gingerbread Man

Mum and Dad decided to have a few days away and so Grandad and Grandma were in charge - yippee! Grandma was senior manager so Grandad had a bit of leeway for fun. But what to do with Aimee, (10), Callum, (9) and Daniel (6)?

You have to be careful not to get out of date and, perhaps, suggest an evening of Peppa Pig when they would rather be playing Minecraft [a very popular online and creative video "game"/ app.]. Consultation suggested a meal at the Gingerbread Man (GM) (other venues are available, but if you know of them let Grandad know please) would go down well. Off we went for a 5pm tea.

The grandchildren had been to GM before, so they were *au fait* with the drill. They soon found somewhere good to sit, and then off we went to order the meals. D. was up for the carvery. A. and C. were keen on the "design your own meal" option which was a great idea, where you could mix and match fish fingers, chips etc but also veggies including mini corn on the cob. Gr. had his usual fish and chips (you can't go wrong with fish and chips). As for drinks, they all knew what they wanted, with fruit juices being popular, Gr. too had a "fruit juice", as Grandma was driving.

It was a great treat to see the children tucking into their chosen repast and beverage. If you want a flexible meal option with junior diners in tow, most times of the day, this is where, locally, you can't go wrong. They are too old for the soft-play area (Jungle Gym) now but that was often a venue for birthday parties where the older generation could sit and relax whilst the children were doing their own wild thing in the jungle.

We had plenty of time after the main course to contemplate the rest of the evening and, as my dad used to say, "let the meal go down", because the desserts were a relaxed time in arriving. Indeed, Gr. was beginning to think they had sent to the Newcastle branch for them.

It was a super, warm evening after a day of rain. The grandchildren were well up for some physical activity and they headed straight for the swings in the garden. Gr. suggested that the trampoline might be a good idea. Only problem, children said, it was full of leaves and acorns. Which, being right underneath an oak tree all winter, indeed it had collected a mass of oak detritus. No problem, Gr. said, let's clean it up. D. was in the lead with a little brush and shovel, and we soon filled two plastic sacks with acorns, leaves and twigs (reminder to self: plant acorns soon). The others joined in with hoovering up the remnants (D.'s idea) and C. busied himself, wiping with a damp cloth. Soon, extraordinary athletic feats were in progress and Gr. took a supervisory seat to watch them and the sunset with another glass, home-made this time, of fruit juice.

51: Out and about

Half-term and the g/children are out and about. The swings in the garden are an attraction and I hear ominous creakings as they swing vigorously to and fro, up and down. They're not little'uns anymore of course and the wooden frame of the swings is protesting. Anxiously check from a distance (and later, closer up) to make sure nothing is about to fall apart and launch them into space. Theoretically, trying to recall school physics, would it be possible for them to swing completely over the top? They can manage about 50 degrees or so at the top of their swing (what's the scientific word for this I wonder - apogee?). Wow, Ca. has a trick where he jumps off the swing at its highest point and flies through the air to land, thankfully, on his feet.

Daniel (aged 6) enthusiastically helps with jobs, fetching buckets for feeding the new calves. He's passionately interested in screen-time, as we call it, playing Minecraft with his cousins or watching YouTube videos. So Grandad and Grandma feel reassured when he wants to do outside things... Such as raiding the polytunnel for seeds. Weeks ago, he purloined a packet of lettuce seeds and one of radishes and headed off to sow them. Like he saw me do, he drew out a furrow in the soil with his finger and emptied the packets of seeds into them. Asking me for labels, he duly marked each row with a label and sticks at either end. As I write, the lettuce are up and the carrots just showing themselves. They are just a tiny bit congested in the row, but we can soon transplant the lettuce and thin out the carrots.

Charlotte (now at secondary school, whilst the others are at Hugo) is very diligent in her studies and proudly comes in to say where she has come in the different exams (quite well). For example, Geography. Grandad wants to know what kinds of questions? Capital cities? (Remember this is first year Geography.) No, Grandad. What then? One of the questions (for six marks) was to discuss the pros and cons of the one-child policy in China. Crikes, Charlotte, that sounds like A-level!

A bit later, Grandad has come back from choir to find Mrs Grandad has possibly been abducted by aliens. But no, she is over the yard, "baby-sitting" (they could be grandad sitting soon). Moseying over, Grandad sees that a full-on dance spectacular is in progress. Yes! Aimee and Ellie both go to Oak Tree Dance Studio (run by Miss Penny) - well it is only a skip and a hop away - and are demonstrating their latest routines to Grandma. What a wonderfully creative and energetic thing!

52: Party time - and some archery

I am writing this in June, and it is the big month for birthday parties. Daniel has his birthday first, and then Aimee has hers, a few days later. I have to rely on Grandma, 'tho., who is diligent in transferring key birthdays in her diary from one year to the next. So, within a few days we are assembled, *toute en famille*, with our cards and prezzies. What to get for these increasingly sophisticated young people? Dad used to ask me that - I used to say - just a piece of paper from the bank, Dad! The little birds whisper that A. is getting keen on horse riding and wants gear for that, whilst D. is really into Lego. You have to admire the Lego designers - how they can make all sorts of shapes from those little plastic blocks - vehicles, people, spacecraft - anything, in fact. And both D. and his brother Callum can make these tremendously complicated models after emptying out the plastic bags full of bricks that the kits come in and searching through them, for the tiniest bits, whilst following the instructions.

Party time! Lovely food, always, and pleasant company. The highlight is the cake. What will the Mums have come up with this time? It's amazing every time! First, a Lego cake with edible bricks, and then - believe it or not - a Pancake Cake. Crikey, how many pancakes did you have to make Mum? (Answer - lots!)

Then it's time for games. The consensus is rounders, especially as one of the presents was a rounders bat and ball. What to use for bases? Farmer Dad has the answer - plastic electric fencing posts. They are easy to put in the ground, white and easy to see, and you can easily "touch base" on them - perfect! Why has no-one thought of this before? Business opportunity for rounders-set makers! Although no-one can ever agree on the finer points of the rules, we all just went for it and had a great time.

Grandma was looking forward to seeing her long-time, nursing friend Sheila who now lives in Oz. She was coming for a whistle-stop one-night stay whilst house-sitting in London for friends. The bonus was that she was bringing her grand-daughter, Sarah (aged 6). Sarah soon got into the swing of things, literally on the swings, and then adored playing on our old mobility scooter that the children use to bomb around the yard on.

But then Daniel (her age) suggested playing with the bows and arrows. Callum (9 now) was brilliant at instructing her what to do and, after initial difficulty, she was soon sending arrows (rubber-tipped, re-enactment arrows) 20 yards or more. She was very proud of her new-found skill and gave us all a giggle by saying "I am really good now and I am going to show C. that I am better than him." There's going to be no "glass ceiling" for her, I predict.

53: Dog show

The annual Ashley Summer Fayre and Dog Show was scheduled a month earlier than usual, and it was a good choice for the sun shone with all its might. Your editor was asked to do his usual and be the commentator. Actually, that is the wrong word possibly because people close to the editor have been wont to say "Commentator? What do you know about dogs?". Fair enough, and I had to explain to them that my role was simply to read out the results of each class: "In reverse order, the results of Class X, the dog most likely to succeed in life, is Butch, with its handler…" You get the idea. It's always a pleasure, even 'though one has to lug public address amplifier, speaker, tent to keep the elements at bay, seat to sit on etc etc.

But I cannot complain this year about the "lugging". No, because grandson Daniel (6, going on a lot more) was super-keen to help. "Can I help, Grandad?" "Of course. D." Grandad, not knowing that a family outing had been planned elsewhere, hereby had caused a bit of a domestic crisis, D. saying flatly he did not want to go with the family but to the Ashley Dog Show; a compromise fortunately was worked out by Mum.)

Reminiscence alert... Grandad thinks back to many church summer fayres over the years - at Birch Church in Manchester - when he responded to the incvitable "call to arms", as in "Scouts are to lay on a stall/sideshow/attraction at the Summer Fayre again this year." Many fond memories of different ideas to get the public to part with their money, including an aerial runway that our Senior Scouts thought would be a good idea, until some unfortunate child got stuck at the top of one of the tallest trees. These things happen, eh?

With the welcome help of my brother Geoff and aforesaid Grandson, we got duly established in our announcement tent and the various classes proceeded as per usual. But where, this year, was the usual class "Six best legs"? This was an invitation for those game enough to display their legs along with those, of course, of their pooch. It had been expunged from the programme. The "Best Biscuit Catcher" class was still there, however - usually won, as this year, by the Pooley-Dents' doggie, who is definitely at Olympic level in this sport.

It was a fabulous day, with significant funds raised for the church upkeep. There's no space here to do justice to all the stalls, like the raffle, plants, bottles, tombola, bric-a-brac, books, teas, burgers, to mention just a few, but it's always a great attraction to have "Bowling for the Pig" (pic.) and we are grateful for the Mayor of Newcastle who presented prizes and the Recharge band who played worship songs. Lots of people made this event possible – to them, THANKS!

54: The long summer holiday

There's a lot of it ahead! Grandad is writing at the beginning of August and the months stretch out ahead. The GCs are in a vacuum left by no daily reason to get up for school, whilst the grown-ups think of it as a continuation of their normal everyday life. What are they to do?

The parents of course are great and book the youngsters into a film for an afternoon, take them away on holiday, or off to riding and other lessons-but it does not seem quite enough! No, back they come for more... more... of what? To be honest, they just love being with one another and doing... "stuff". Such as?

Gr. was reading on the patio, watching the grandchildren playing. The five of them kept linking arms and looking down. What were they playing? It turned out to be ... "monkey football". The finer points, I must admit, of this eluded me. Although I thought that they must have invented it, Google explains – check it out!

Yet that wasn't enough....

A conversation:
  "Grandad"
  "Yes"
  "Can we earn some money? We want jobs to do."

Grandad weighs up how much it is going to cost him whilst possible getting some useful jobs done around the homestead.

"Tell you what, I will pay you £1 for every bucket-full of weeds you bring me."

This turns out to be a good plan because off go the five of them (book idea? - Famous Five Go Weeding) disappear with gloves and buckets to pull up nasty weeds from Grandad's allotment. Yippee!

If you want a team of enthusiastic youngsters to do some jobs - just let me know. (Hmm - better apply for a gangmaster's licence.)

55: Back to school and more Messy Church

A family tradition is that when the children have got their school clothes on for the first day back, they line up by the gate and we take a picture. We have those for our boys and now their children are duly taking their turn. This time we have Aimee, dressed in her very smart new, secondary-school uniform, whilst her older cousin Charlotte is going into Year 2 at her "big" school. Ellie, Callum and Daniel are all spruced up on the photo, heading back to Hugo Meynell.

Grandad was keen to replace the mobility scooter that we had inherited from step-mum Eleanor. After some five years of acting as a general-purpose vehicle for all the children to tear round the yard on, it finally lost its whoompf. The helpful mobility shop in Drayton had a very old one, described as the classic car of mobility scooters; it went like a bomb, so is now installed as the new children's "4x4". The old one did marvellously - somehow, they managed to get 7 children on it once, with visiting cousins keen to take part.

Messy Church resumed after the holiday break. My call went out to grandchildren (GC) for the September one. "We're coming, Grandad!" Off we went, Daniel, Callum and me. No messing about, they were well into putting chairs and tables out. "We know where everything is, Grandad!" In next to no time, the room was ready.

Vicar Terry needed no persuasion to get into one of the craft activities (making hieroglyphic bookmarks - it was an Egyptian theme, around the Bible story of Joseph and his Dreamcoat). And the game later was "Mummies" – wrapping everyone in toilet paper.

Daniel was on the ball and quick to point out that no-one was making sandwiches. "We need to be on that stall, Grandad!" Grandad did not want to steal anyone's thunder - "Who's on the catering team today, Jean?" "Err... you!" Off we went to attack the ham sandwich production line. Daniel and Callum were well up for this and soon mastered the art of washing hands first and then buttering the bread ("No islands, boys!", as Grandad learnt at scout camp years ago) and putting ham slices in place.

Photos taken, everything packed up and no mess left – not-Messy Church restored!

56: Christmas with Sandra

Writing this in mid-January, Christmas is now a memory, but a great time to reflect on super times with our two sets of grandchildren and their parents. Now that the grandchildren are older of course they are spending more and more time doing their own thing and less and less time with Grandad. No longer "Please can we go in the workshop Grandad?" or "Can we go down to the pond?" The lure of different screens is strong, not to mention homework, school friends and other interests.

Aimee (she's now at secondary school) had, from Santa Claus, a disembodied head. It is a "hair-dressing training head". Grandad does not like horror movies and stuff, so he was discombobulated to see this decapitated object staring at him when he went in for Christmas Eve celebrations at next door. It came with some sort of clamp to fix it firmly to the table, all the more designed to terrify Grandad with her glassy eyes. She is called "Sandra" but that makes her no more human. She is better from behind, because then all you see is her hair. Is "she" going to be there? Grandad has to ask himself, before venturing into next-door.

A.'s brothers had more light-hearted Christmas gifts. Amazingly, "Play People" are still around (or that's what they looked like). I remember Play People from almost 50 years ago when we bought them for their dad. So how heartening to see them here again. Daniel. had an amazing aeroplane for the Play People to ride in, which you can take to pieces and re-assemble. Oh, and he also had a guitar, which promises lots of fun concerts later.

Callum had an electronic drum kit, which is really good for the punch-line of jokes, as in: "Knock Knock who's there?" Doctor - Doctor Who. - Yes, you said it. BOOM BOOM". Callum, like Daniel, also likes construction kits - fantastic Lego but also electronic circuits that you can put together without need for soldering iron. Marvellous fun.

Do they still believe in Father Christmas you may want to ask. Such a thorny issue with children of different ages. "Miracle on 42nd Street" is on every year, so we can reflect on the nature of belief in unseen-figures whilst watching that. The film shows adults not prepared to accept that Santa exists at one level, whilst at the same time refusing to say he doesn't and thus spoil Christmas for the children. In the end, everyone agrees he is real. Thank goodness!

57: Carry on whistling!

I hope I didn't freak anyone out with my description last month of grand-daughter Aimee's Christmas present of a "hairdressing styling head", called "Sandra". I am NOT going to include a photo of same. Truly, I cannot look at it without shivering. So, clearly, it's best if she ("Sandra") can be turned to face the wall when Grandad is going into next door.

What I didn't mention last month was the scene at the other grandchildren's house, which is opposite us, as opposed to next door. Charlotte is now a teenager, in her second year of secondary school, so she is difficult to track down, and (worse still) to induce her to write more poems for the magazine, but I am working on it. She does things which cannot easily be featured easily in this column, such as playing football for a local team, and swimming in galas (her dad has complained that she can beat him now). Taking after your editor and her other grandparents John and Rhiannon, she is also finding languages interesting and is studying German and French at school.

Her sister, Ellie, continues with her dancing at, of course, the Blore Heath's own school of dance - Oak Tree Dance Studio, run by "Miss Penny" and her team. She's always loved dancing and has often given us private dance shows, along with other drama performances from her sister and cousins. They are great fun, and we always get privileged seats, on the front row of the living room of course. Whilst "Sandra" gives me the creeps, E.'s current craze is an "app." on her phone that lets you distort people's faces into grotesque shapes. To be precise, it makes one's mouth / lips totally bizarre. For some reason, rather than this being horrifying, it is funny!

Oh, I forgot to mention Christmas dinners. By some feat of inspiration, daughter-in-law Caroline managed to get some Christmas crackers that included a set of whistles. They are tuned to different notes and, included, is a sheet of "music". It reminded me of years ago when we Scouts used to do handbell recitals. It was a sudden fad of our scoutmaster who wrote the "music" on rolls of wallpaper. Each bell had a number according to a musical scale, and you donged your bell when your number came up. I can still remember the tune for English Country Garden (5,7,1,3,2,4 etc). These whistles were on the same lines - you blew your whistle when your number came up. Everyone took it seriously and we managed in end to produce reasonably tuneful renditions of popular tunes.

Anyone want to book us for a whistle-stop tour?

58: Flicks and dinner after

How lucky we are to still have a cinema in Market Drayton. When I was little, we could go to the posh cinema at the end of Dickenson Road in Manchester (only five minutes' walk). It had an "ABC Minors" show on a Saturday morning. But then it burned down, leaving only the "fleapit" (but it wasn't that bad, just what we called it.) - the "Trocadero", scene of teenage trysts. But I digress...

We were down to be baby-sitting (of course, they are not babies!). What to do? Thankfully, the three "next-door" grandchildren, Aimee, Callum and Daniel, were well up to the occasion and came with games and puzzles to occupy bored grandparents. We quite liked one game, "Guess Who?" where you had to guess what the other person had on their board from descriptions.

Then, it was off to Market Drayton to see the new "Mary Poppins". Grandad (and possibly Callum and Daniel) thought that this could be too soppy for words but kept his views to himself. In the event, it wasn't all that bad. The dance sequences (lamplighters, not chimney sweeps) were very impressive, relying not just on digital special effects, but on real talent with excellent choreography.

Afterwards, we all repaired to the Gingerbread Man, which is the preferred venue for our grandchildren's celebration meals. In case you have not been there, you need to go for the CARVERY, which seems to be available most days and nights from early to late. You choose whether to have a small, medium or large plate and pay accordingly. Our g/children always have medium (adult!) plates with extra pigs-in-blankets and soon woof the lot down. Grandad's appetite is smaller now, so he secretes some of his meat slices in a napkin to eat later. A bit gross but, shsss, don't tell, will you?

PS The adult-sized plates just don't quite cut the mustard for ours, 'cos there needs to be "afters" as well. Ice cream sundaes and chocolate brownies are the order of the day. Very reasonable in price and scrumptious.

See you there one day?

59: Wandering minstrels

It's half-term. A fruitful time for encounters with the g/children, as they find new projects whilst not at school.

Knock-knock. The Wordsworth's-head-door-knocker on our front door was in action. (It was a kind gift from a graduate student, remembering my fondness for he of The Daffodils).

Outside the door, Charlotte and Ellie, carrying stuff - a guitar and a small noticeboard.

"Hello Grandad and Grandma, would you like to hear our song?"

"Of course, in you come." Grandma and self take up positions, ready for the recital. Charlotte is at the piano, Ellie perched, folk-singer like, with her guitar and footstool. They explain that they have just put the act together. Charlotte picks out the tune on the piano, Ellie accompanies, and they sing. Grandad cannot work out whether they had just made the song up or it was a "cover" of a well-known modern song that he had not heard *. Half-way through, Charlotte jumps off the piano stool and beats out a rhythm on the noticeboard they had brought with them, whilst Ellie claps along. Clearly, they had worked the rhythm out in some detail because it was quite ornate. The song over, they take a bow, and disappear back, *chez eux*.

Grandad/ma were double-booked for the Irish Night ceilidh at the Memorial Hall so took Callum and Dan along there instead of young-person-sitting at home. Callum was already very tired and went into sleep-mode, but Daniel was all-eyes for the band and the dancing and clapped enthusiastically along with everyone else. The soda bread on the table went down a treat, especially with the butter, but that meant they weren't hungry by the time the meal came. The jury's out on whether they "enjoyed" it, but it was a great new experience.

`* It was both, Grandad has since found out.

60: Solar lights can give you sunburn

It's Good Friday and a super-hot day. The g/children are out and about early and come to our side to play rounders. They're pretty good at it and the five of them play together until there is just a tiny falling-out and one disappears inside.

Mrs Grandad has been tempted by the closing-down-sale-everything-must-go at Homebase. Grandma comes home with solar lights for the garden. What a bargain - the box says 43 metres in length. Wow. There are indeed metres and metres of them, with tiny LEDs on a long, thin copper wire. The wire needs careful unrolling to stop it tangling ... anyhow, an hour later, in the hot sun, with Rosie and me on the job, they are unravelled and strung along a fence (good job we have lots of them round and about). If I get sunburn, it's down to those solar lights...

The day still hot, the G/children decide on a water fight. All sorts of equipment come into play, but it has to be said that a bucket of water hurled against opponents is more primitively satisfying than a high-tech-looking water cannon. Grandad stayed well away - five against one isn't fair. They round off the day with a game of badminton in the garden. It is so good to see them all playing together - as long as there are no more fall-outs.

Finally, the children draw in chalk a complicated network of roads on the yard and drive round them on their scooters, bikes and the mobility scooter. I think I told you about this. We had inherited one from my stepmother Eleanor, and the children loved to zoom round on it. But eventually it wore out and I traded it in for a much bigger (although old-fashioned) model, described as the Rolls Royce of mobility scooters). It can do 6 mph which is pretty fast. They have a lot of fun on it, even taking it across the fields. Best of all is to tow something behind - like a toy tractor and come whizzing down the drive. Watch out Grandad - the tractor has no brakes!

Messy Church for Easter happened last week; the whole of Hugo School came by coach to church, where a squad of church volunteers welcomed them. There were crafts, singing led by Peter Shone, and a talk from Jean Buckley.

New idea - Open the Book. Using specially created material by The Bible Society, church volunteers will be visiting Hugo and Mucklestone schools to read bible stories. More on this in later issues of the Magazine. If you feel you can help, contact Denise Keen.

61: A school year ending

It's end of term for the young ones and that means - exam time. Ellie has SATS to prepare for at Hugo and is thinking about secondary school. Charlotte has end-of-second-year (already!?) tests, and there's more tests for Callum at Hugo and end-of-year ones for Aimee at The Grove. On top of all this, Ellie has sat ballet exams (and did well) and is rehearsing for a big part in the end of year musical at Hugo.

But what about leisure? Aimee is loving horse riding (shhh, she wants her own gee-gee!). Callum is well into an obscure computer game where he is online with his friend (he plays "real" football as well). Charlotte always looks ace in her football kit. Ellie dances several times a week. Oh, and she just popped in to show Grandma a dress she had suddenly decided to make out of a pillowcase (it looks great on her). Daniel just the other day learned to ride his two-wheeler with Dad's help (we won't mention the crashes but really he should not try riding through narrow gates). And the boys have been going on quite long walks with Dad and Uncle Matthew - and even enjoying them!

Daniel is nearly 8. Daniel is really enthusiastic about Messy Church and remembers the dates and times. Grandad loves taking him. But he eschews the activities. Daniel is not "into" activities. He wants to work. At the last Messy Church he and I were assigned to catering. Along with George, an ex-Beaver, we were a great team laying out the sandwiches supplied by George's mum and dad and serving drinks. The little lads (and they are only 7/8 years old) were a great asset to Grandad.

Anyhow, Daniel, in church at Messy Church, was really interested in where Grandad sits during choir and said he would like to come. Wow! He was up bright and early on the Sunday ("8.55, Daniel!"). He sat with Grandad in the choir stalls and everyone made a real fuss of him. He knew the first hymn from school, followed the service quite well and sang along with some of the other hymns on this "Family Communion" morning. Grandad was so pleased, feeling perhaps the continuation of a family heritage: Grandad's dad Bob Hegarty, and paternal grandad William were very committed church-goers. Is there a gene for church-going?

62: French conversation, a trouser and a new arrival

Can you help me with my French homework? That's what Charlotte comes to ours with. Grandad has a little tremor of dread - Charlotte is coming on so fast with "French" that maybe Grandad cannot "comprendre". She has a bundle of good-old-fashioned index cards. Her "devoirs" - homework - was to prepare a dialogue between her and a friend, with question and answer. Grandad plays the part of her friend, asking various questions in French, such as: "What did you do today", "What are you going to do tomorrow?" Charlotte had written out the questions and the answers on the cards so it was pretty easy for Grandad. It was fun to have this conversation with Charlotte!

These days we are all assailed with accusations of not being gender-neutral. You can't say that something is for girls or boys or vice versa. No! That is "gender-ist". Nevertheless, you might think that sewing is for girls, more than boys. But, here on the farm, Daniel comes with Aimee and Ellie to do some dressmaking/tailoring with Grandma. He is interested in the sewing machine and Grandma lets him sew two lengths of fabric together.

Grandad, bored, goes off to his office to do some editing of the Magazine. Suddenly, in comes Daniel. In his super-polite voice, he says "Excuse me Grandad, please can I measure you?" I stand up and he puts a tape measure around ... my thigh. I said nothing, what do I know?   "I am making you some trousers, Grandad."

"Don't you want to know how long my leg is?"

"No, Grandad." [see why, below!]

I am 46 something or other and off he goes. A little later, my trouser (note singular) appears.

"Here you are, Grandad."

"How do I wear it, Daniel?" [He tells me to tuck the "trouser" into the waistband of my current trousers.]

"Well, that is just super, Daniel, Thanks,"

Grandad now has a "trouser", well, strictly, half of a trouser as he had not sewed the sides together. I complain that it is too long. "Don't worry, Grandad." He appears with a wicked-looking pair of scissors and proceeds to chop off the excess fabric from the bottom of my trouser. He has a future as a tailor! Grandad has to re-conceptualise this chic, *nouvelle-couture*. He searches his memory banks - "chaps" surfaces. You know, like cowboys wore in the wild west to protect their jeans from thistles and thorns. But Daniel thinks, "knee pad". For my gardening. OK!   "Daniel, please can you make me another for my other leg?"

"No problem, Grandad!"

70

63: Nancy – and a murder mystery play.

We were all excited to meet Nancy. She is a Welsh cob and looks absolutely splendid. She has her own paddock and a room in the barn as well. Not having had equines before, Grandad was amazed to see how much grass she could eat; and, not to put too fine a point on it, how much came out at the other end. All the better for Grandad's allotment.

The summer holiday started for Grandad with the Starship Discovery Holiday Bible Club. With Ellie as assistant, Grandad was in charge of games. Callum came too and enjoyed the mix of activities. But not, he said, the dancing. Dancing? Grandad queried. He meant the worship songs such as "My Lighthouse" which have actions appropriate to the words.

Midweek, we were invited to afternoon tea. Outside, were tables and chairs, all beautifully laid out. It was scorching hot but we didn't mind as we were poured juice and offered crisps and similar. Sandwiches came out of the fridge, and then there were chocolate buns, home-made by the team. Could we have the recipe for the Magazine, Grandad wanted to know... the answer was yes so look out for this in a forthcoming issue.

Next day, whoops of delight issued from the garden. The children were launching themselves down a slope on small, inflatable mattresses. Further inspection revealed a water-slide, spotted in a nearby shop by Aimee. You attached a hose to it, and then the water came out along the length of the slide through small holes. You could then "surf" down the slide. Grandad suggested they should put some washing-up liquid on it. This certainly improved the downhill speed and they were soon surfing over the end of the slide. Great fun. "Does Grandad want a go?" asked Mum Caroline. (Yes I did but didn't want to break the slide).

"You are invited to a play tonight." Charlotte had master-minded the writing and rehearsals. There was much anticipation among the grown-ups. It was a mystery-thriller. Sacred to a secret cult, a jewelled necklace was unknowingly bought by a lady (Charlotte), shopping with a friend (Aimee), who was then murdered by a cult-follower (Callum, with black cloak and make-up). A police inspector (Ellie, suitably dressed in a suit) then interviewed the lady's friend on suspicion of the murder. End of Act 1.

We don't know when the play will continue (especially as it hasn't yet been written) and we are all wondering how it will end. We all marvelled at this gem of a drama that had been created in a day. There were scene changes, costumes, make-up and slick dialogue. What was Daniel's part, you may wonder. He was Master of Ceremonies, announcing the start of the play, and then holding up signs (made by Aimee), to tell us where each scene was taking place. The only fly in the ointment was Grandad's movie camera playing-up - was that the curse of the necklace at work?

64: Have wheels, will travel - mostly.

Readers may remember that Grandad encouraged the g/children to use the mobility scooter inherited from Eleanor (step-mum). I recall the time when Callum, aged about 5, sat on the scooter for the first time, stored in one of our farm buildings; I showed him how to make it move. Wow! That was a eureka! moment. You can imagine his excitement. He soon learned to do a three-point turn, and after that he was off. It was quite safe, with a low centre-of-gravity. Of course, the other children soon cottoned on, and it was much in demand as fun transport up and down our farm drive. (See diary entry no. 5.) Time went on, and it got worn-out. Conversations with the helpful mobility shop in Drayton (that I was looking for fun transport for the grandchildren) suggested there was just the job lurking at the back of a shed somewhere. This resulted in the acquisition of a "Sungift 200", which was described as the "Rolls Royce of mobility scooters". A two-speed option offered 6 mph (fast walking speed is 4 mph) top speed. Since it came, with its two powerful batteries and rugged construction, it's been in great demand by all five of the g/children and their cousins and friends.

But alas. A week ago it ceased to respond to commands. It seemed to be defunct. It was a non-mobility scooter. All Grandad's ideas about how to revive it failed to work. It needed a visit from Geoff, Grandad's technically skilled brother. When he came, it was top-of-the-list for his attentions. First, he found a blown fuse. Replacing it did not produce mobility. And so, open-heart explorations were required. All to no avail - without a wiring diagram, Geoff was exploring blind. Then, after a refreshing sleep on his last night at Blore Heath, he was all up for more investigations into the difficult-to-access back end, where the motor and other wiring resided.

Close observation and Geoff's technical intuition suggested shorting out a microswitch that could be the problem. Re-assembly. Success! Forward and backwards motion was effected!

The children and their cousins and friends have, in the past few days, really given the machine some stick. As well as zooming up and down the drive with one person driving (obviously that's what it's designed for), they like to see how many they can get on at one time (pic.) . The limit seems to be four: one steering, standing up, one sitting in the footwell, one on the seat facing backwards, one sitting on top of the person on the seat (pic). Grandad suggested adding the little, four-wheeled garden trailer. That adds another dimension, so they can be seen setting off on a mini-safari round the allotment and up the lane (pic). Happy days! Maybe if I got another one ... races?

66: Online auction site comes to the rescue

Last month I told how the grandchildren's mobility scooter / "4x4" was repaired. Well, sad to say, it not long after decided to make sounds like gravel was in its gear box and give up the ghost. Once again, it was a non-mobility scooter. Grandad decided that surely there must be another one somewhere and promptly looked on that well-known online auction site. "Blow me down" said Grandad to himself, when up popped the exact same model for sale at a quite reasonable price. Only problem - "buyer collects from Norwich". Undeterred, Grandad puts in a really low offer and surprisingly finds himself the buyer.

One of the delights that we can offer the g/children is a visit to a local hostelry, the Ginger Bread Man (other places to feed g/c are available). As I reported in previous diary entries, this has a very reasonable carvery at most times of the day/week and it is a very popular venue for "our lot". The boys in particular can demolish an adult-sized portion very easily. This could be, for example, slices of turkey, several vegetables, "pigs in blankets", Yorkshire puds, gravy and a bottle of juice.

Daniel had clearly enjoyed a massive portion and asked whether he could have dessert.　　"Aren't you full up?" asked the grown-ups.

Answer - "Well my main course-pipe is full up, but my dessert pipe is empty."

D. has joined the Hugo school choir and will be singing with the Community Choir this Sunday in "Captain Noah and his Floating Zoo", a really fun cantata written by Michael Flanders (he of the Hippotamus Song and "I'm a gnu", which readers of a certain age will remember from Children's Favourites).

Charlotte has moved into 3rd year at Newport and is keen on languages and swimming. Ellie enjoys dancing at the Oak Tree Dance studio and was really active in the Holiday Bible Club. Aimee loves getting to know her pony Nancy, whilst the boys Callum and Daniel are into video games and Lego.

Grandad has been helping with "Open the Book" (see elsewhere in this Diary) and wears the "biblical" costume that Viv (thanks for all your work on the costumes) has made for him and the other members of the Open the Book team. Grandad likes to think of himself as a "scribe" at the Open the Book readings, but he was brought down to earth by Daniel relaying a classmate's comment about him, the narrator:　　"Is that your Grandad....or your Grandma?"

66: Climbing walls.

Soon we move into another decade and of course one wonders what it will hold for our g/children. Maybe they will even have seen Brexit!

But back to the present, November 1, as I write this diary. Half-term has finished for our "famous five" and they will be back at school on Monday. Hallowe'en was yesterday and I don't remember them being so excited. Callum has been visiting us daily to update us on his costume for "trick and treating". He decided to go as "The grim reaper". He got a cloak and a cowl and scary slippers (pic. left) and impatiently awaited his (plastic) scythe. Ellie and Charlotte came to trick and treat us (pic. right).

Keen to find a treat for all five of the g/children, Rosie suggested a trip to "Climbing the Walls" in Shrewsbury.

They were up for that. Ellie and Charlotte had been there before but Aimee, Daniel and Callum hadn't. You pay for an hour on the different climbing walls and parents can watch from a balcony. There are instructors on hand and everyone has to wear a harness. These are attached to a mysterious thing in the ceiling (like an inertia seat belt) so you can just throw yourself off the wall and gently descend. There are pretty awesome walls for children/beginners and then terrifying ones for grown-ups who shin up with dangly things on their belts (karabiners) and loops of rope.   Callum was always a great one for climbing, even when he was tiny, and was always shinning up gates or whatever when Grandad let him on a trip round the farm. So he was really in his element. Aimee was fine, but Dan was a tad apprehensive (like G/dad would be) and needed quite a bit of encouragement to have a go.

It was great to watch them gain more and more confidence on the various walls. Grandad kept trying to find suitable puns for the occasion but couldn't think of any - which was slowly driving him up the wall.

67: Screens

The new year starts and the grandchildren are recovering from all the excitement of Christmas. Grandparents are worried about all the press coverage of research into the bad effects of too much screen-time, but there is no easy answer. There is homework to do, needing research on the internet (Charlotte). Then there is socialising, with young teens catching up on what their friends are doing (Aimee and Ellie). Not to mention catching up on the latest developments in video gaming on Fortnite (Callum), a social activity in itself with friends. And keeping abreast of online farming (Daniel). All of them require looking at screens (and Grandad is writing this on a screen as well!).

But, hey, I am over-simplifying, because all the g/children are doing all kinds of things. There is swimming, dancing, football, horse-riding, farming and much more besides. Grandad and Grandma cannot easily keep pace with everything that is going on!

Grandad continues to work (half-time now) as lecturer in psychology at Keele Uni. Actually, he is "Father of the House", as the oldest employee. "How long have you worked here?" people ask. I say, "Well there were dinosaurs in the Keele woods when I came." (Hah hah!) Students are 18+ years old, mostly. Without exception, they have smart phones and usually Apple laptops as well. Unbelievably to Grandad they are reading scientific articles online, which appear to be microscopically small on their smartphone screens. It won't be all that long before our Charlotte (14 now) will be at Uni too!

Having said all that, guess what made Christmas Day and Boxing Day, a resounding success? MONOPOLY! After lovely eats and sharing the children's excitement over presents from Santa, they got out the game. This is the first Christmas for quite a while that we have played a table game as a family, so it was special. We all enjoyed it, especially "Grandma Anne" (Aimee, Callum and Dan's Grandma), who won the first game resoundingly. But the excitement proved too much for Grandma Rosie who went to bed super-early!

Grandad has not had a lot of success hitherto with mobile phones. No. The house-elves have spirited several of the (non-smart) ones away. Thank goodness for the helpful people at the second-hand phone shop in 'Drayton, who can be relied on to find a replacement fairly cheaply. Grandad recently decided he needed a proper smartphone (well, everyone else seems to have them) and seemed to make the shop's day by investing in quite an expensive one. So, watch out, house-elves - I think I have out-smarted you this time.

68: Grandad has a cold

Grandad has only just emerged from an horrendous dose of a cold. To call it that, however, seems too mild. There has to be a worse name for what laid me really low. It comes every year, just before Christmas - starting with a sore throat and then - wham - the Full-Monty of a chest infection etc etc. Thankfully no-one *chez nous* seems to have had it as bad. Grandad even missed the candle-lit carol service at church, without which Christmas is less of a special event.

Christmas, apart from that, was pretty good. We enjoyed all the grandchildren's toys and loved, especially, playing Monopoly (see Diary, No. 67). What did Santa Claus bring them you might be wondering? I'm afraid the appeal of presents for young teenage girls (Aimee) evaded me so I can't help you there. Callum really needed a bigger screen for his beloved computer games, and Santa obliged. Daniel received two radio-controlled model cars. They were great fun and they whizzed around the room. One remembers presents in former years that did not always perform as expected, or broke down, or needed batteries when the shops were shut. But these were really good and did not even break when they collided with table legs.

The g/children "opposite" also had super presents but I'll have to tell you about those next time. Oh, but I am forgetting sumptuous Christmas dinner - a joint effort between the families. Occasion of course for reminiscing, for example when Grandad decided one year that the pudd. would definitely come in flaming, as in the adverts. But he overdid the high-octane, Romania-purchased spirit, which obliged by bursting into flames, made the dish red-hot, whereupon Grandad promptly let it drop. Beware too much spirit-of-Christmas!

Daughter-in-law Caroline had, a couple of years before, got some crackers which had small whistles in them, each with a musical pitch, and numbered. A sheet of "music" was also provided. [See Diary no. 57 for more on this.] Everyone had a whistle and was supposed to blow their whistle when their number comes up. This is now a fixture at festive meals. The musically-ambitious amongst the group hope that everyone will not only blow their whistle at the appointed time but also observe some semblance of the tempo. (Even Jingle Bells is unrecognisable if there are long gaps between some of the notes and others come too quickly.) After a bit of a rehearsal we sometimes surprised ourselves with a passing rendition.

Now they are back at school and everything has gone quiet. Roll on Easter hols.

69: Bat stew

The "five" (Charlotte 14, Aimee 12, Ellie 11, Callum 10, Daniel 8) were with us for tea whilst parents were away doing their own thing. What would they like to eat? Suggestions of Shepherd's pie, bangers and mash, cheese on toast did not find favour. "What do you really like?" The reply PIZZAS, accompanied by big smiles and general happiness, seemed to be the clincher. Thus it was, and the one remaining parent duly disappeared to order same from a well-known chain with the unlikely name of darts or cribbage or some pub game like that.

If you have not got g/children aged 8-14 with a passion for pizzas, we could do a deal and rent ours out - just get in touch. They sat round our round table and were *aux anges* as the French say [with the angels - i.e. very happy] as they munched away. Afterwards, they engaged in chat and friendly banter, whereupon the talk got round to the news on coronavirus. Daniel sometimes tends to be put down by the older ones. But he has an assertive voice and so his opinions on the pestilence were clearly heard. "Bat stew." That was his considered view on the cause of the outbreak. "What do you mean?" we asked. Standing up, he proclaimed, in no uncertain terms: "BAT STEW - DO NOT EAT BAT STEW." Finger wagging, one had to be impressed, and Grandad for one will definitely NOT be eating bat stew from now on.

Being a former cub leader (Akela) no less, Grandad is really chuffed that Daniel has joined Ashley Cub Scouts. The April magazine had a report on what Cubs are getting up to, and it is really impressive. They have not only been doing lots of fun things but raising lots of money for social causes - national and international. He was "invested" the other evening. Grandad was proud to see him make the "Scout Sign", to say his Cub Scout Promise and receive his 1st Ashley Air Scouts neckerchief. G/dad was nostalgic, as he was Akela for many years and invested many Ashley youngsters.

The Promise and Law remain and are ideals to which we all should aspire: "I promise that I will do my best. To do my duty to my God and the Queen. To help other people and to keep the Cub Scout Law." The Law: Cub Scouts always do their best, think of others before themselves, and do a good turn every day."

70: Black chalk and kites

Grandad likes to browse YouTube videos on farming, gardening and DIY. Most of them are from the US where enthusiastic (often bearded) blokes demonstrate their skills, or cunning tricks for getting thorny problems solved. Such as how to pull out a tree root or extract the remains of a rotten fence post. Quite a few are on the subject of making charcoal. The attraction of home charcoal making is not easily apparent, I must say. The videos show that to produce enough lumpwood charcoal for a barbeque requires quite a lot of wood and time and apparatus. As one comment said, "All that, when you can buy the stuff at a garage!" Anyhow, the idea appeals, especially when you have lots of wood and space to experiment, so I had a go on a very small scale.

The principle of charcoal making is to burn wood without oxygen. It ends up as charred wood that has several properties. You can draw with it if you are artistic. Or if you set it alight (as for a BBQ) it burns without much smoke and with a lot of heat. What I did was to get an old biscuit tin, bash four holes in the lid with a nail, put in some pieces of willow of different thicknesses, and then put it in a small bonfire. If you watch, steam comes out of the holes and then flame. This flame is wood gas, which has been produced commercially to power cars for example. After not very long, I let the can cool down and—hey presto—the wood had turned to charcoal! Quite satisfying.

I went to share my success with the grandchildren. "What is it Grandad?" They wanted to know. Mum Becky said, "It's like black chalk, you can draw with it." This must have fired up their imagination for, a short time later, they were all sitting cross-legged on our yard drawing on the flagstones with said "black chalk". They had decided to play an outdoor version of "Pictionary".

Grandad had a birthday the other week and of course had to have a party just like the Grandchildren get. I said I would like a cake with Cadbury's Flakes on (my fav. chocolate) ["only the crumbliest, flakeyist chocolate tastes like chocolate never tasted before", who says advertising doesn't work?] as well as some home-made blackcurrant ice cream (thanks, Rosie). I wanted some games and Rosie suggested buying the children some kites. Ordering online got them here in a couple of days and making them occupied the youngsters for quite a while. We could not fly them there and then because it was far too windy but the following two nights kite flying was very successful.

Callum decided he needed to go inside so he got the tractor to fly his kite for him whilst he was away. It did quite well, keeping it in the air for ages.

71: What goes up

Last month I told you about my birthday party and the fun we all had with kites. Of course, you are at the mercy of the wind. Here at Blore Heath we never lack for wind which of course is great for kites. Although you can have too much of a good thing. The night of my birthday it was blowing literally a gale. If you have flown kites in blustery weather you will know what happens—the kite ducks and dives all over the place, rather than ascending serenely into the heavens, as with a steady wind.

My brother Geoff was intrigued by model aeroplanes from a young age. Dad built him one out of balsa wood and tissue paper reinforced by "size". Male readers of a certain age will no doubt remember that was a popular hobby in the 1950s (perhaps it still is?) although your editor never had the patience to stick all those bits of balsa wood together. Anyhow, Dad did, and we proudly took his model off to Birch Park to fly it. Unfortunately, and I still feel guilty about this, it flew too well and ended up in a tall tree. How to get it down? We simply couldn't—and bits of it might still be there. Dad was very patient and understanding but it was a great shame.

I mention this now because I bought a modern model plane online, intending to play with the grandchildren. It was made of a foam material and actually had an online engine that you charged up from a battery. There was a radio control unit too. I took it out with Callum and Daniel to fly but it was not very successful at flying and went round and round in circles before doing a nosedive.

Anyhow, I thought to myself to see if I could get it to fly properly and took it into one of our fields one evening, when there was hardly any wind (or so I thought, wind force being partly a function of altitude). It still misbehaved. But then I twiddled a knob called "trim" (my brother had said that the wrong trim might be the problem) and let it fly on full throttle (remote radio control remember). Wow, that did the trick. Up and up it went and I was pretty impressed. It was not obviously under the control of the radio "control" (but that might have been pilot inexperience) but it happily flew higher and higher in graceful circles. But, in the words of the prophet as they say, what goes up … the onboard battery charge failed, and it fell downwards, right into the middle of a thick hedge. It's still there because I could not get at it for the brambles and hawthorn. It won't rot so maybe at hedge cutting time it might re-appear.

I've bought another one. This time I am going to wait for brother Geoff to give me some pointers on radio control flying (he used to be in a club). But I've a funny feeling that there might be a sense of déjà vu...

72: Headless wonders

With parents temporarily away, we were privileged to be hosts to the grand-children for the evening. Of course, the central event was pizzas from a local, well-known provider of same with the unlikely name of Cribbage or some such parlour game. These duly arrived with "dips" and "skins" and very tasty too. Grandad likes a pizza especially with little fishes on. And chips.

Pizzas consumed it was time for chat and activities. Grandad had arranged for an activity—from an American company. They supply each month a project—be it more technical or creative, you choose—for children of different ages to do. This month it was to build a model "ballista", an "ancient military siege engine in the form of a crossbow", Wikipedia says. Concentration and application produced it and a few balls were shot at the targets supplied. But this was tame stuff. The party needed to come alive. Cue collective ideas of the Famous Five!

Out came Grandad's video camera and thus there had to be some kind of film to make, a drama to enact. Out of somewhere, I don't know, came the

disembodied head with HAIR that Grandad really does not like—it gives him the screaming heeby-jeebies. Earlier diary entries refer. Callum swung it round and round by its hair like a triumphant executioner.

Charlotte then decided to pull her woollen hoodie over her head and somehow attach said head. Now this took some time while she and Ellie worked out how to get the effect they wanted. This was pretty scary but also extremely funny and we all laughed at the antics. But, wait, more was to come, as the video camera was at the ready. Quite a lot of time went by whilst brainstorming on a suitable video plot took place. Finally, what emerged was a horror story. Aimee would be the evil collector of heads and Callum her collector-accomplice. Grandad and Charlotte had to position themselves so that only their heads were visible above the armchairs. The scary head was the "latest acquisition". The video was duly made.

Copies of video available for small fee, just contact the author. 18+ only.

73: Mr Al-Jabr

Wandering next door to cadge a cuppa, Grandad was assailed by Callum proclaiming he had finished his homework. He was excited because he usually left it to the last minute, so he was dead chuffed that he had got ahead of himself. It seemed that he had stacks of the stuff to do—five pieces in all—and he has only just started secondary school!

Grandad wanted to know what he had to do. One was for RE—religious education. He had to fill in a grid of the letters of the alphabet with the names of religious figures or concepts. Yes, he had done this—so well done Callum. The internet had come to his help, as it does every month for Grandad.

Next was an essay on which books he liked to read. Then there was another grid—of sums. It seemed to be a "placement test" to see what level he was at, mathematically speaking. Some were straightforward and Grandad could see they were correct. Others were a bit tricky for Grandad but Callum had got most of them right. But he had left blanks. Some were of the kind "Solve: $3x+ 2= 8$".

Grandad had a major flashback. When he was Callum's age (just a short while ago) he was introduced to algebra by teacher Mr Bromley [how can one remember his name from 63 years ago- have not thought about him 'til now??] and hadn't the foggiest. Perplexed he was and Dad was away. Mum found a retired headmistress who lived down the road (Hall Road, Rusholme, Manchester 14 - it is still there). In 20 minutes, she had shown your editor how to solve a linear equation. What relief, so simple when explained one-to-one.

Now come on readers, many of you have had a state secondary education. Can you solve that equation (= "find the value of x")? Some 60 years on, Grandad had forgotten the method so clearly shown by the teacher down the road. This time, YouTube to the rescue, where he found the modern equivalent of that kind headmistress. It's a he—on Google - "Math Antics". He explains things really well, not just what to do but why.

Grandad wondered who had invented this particular form of secondary school torture. Apparently, it was a certain Muhammad ibn Musa al-Khwarizmi who was a 9th-century Muslim mathematician and astronomer. He is known as the "father of algebra", a word derived from the title of his book, *Kitab al-Jabr*. Amazingly, you can "read" (check it out to see why I have put this in inverted commas) this book yourself all these centuries on, courtesy of the internet. If you cannot understand it, you are on the same camel as Grandad, so not to bother contacting me please to explain it.

74: Zooming around

Christmas seems a long way off now but every time I go next door Callum is zooming around. No, I don't mean that ever-more-popular online meeting thingy; for Callum had something altogether more exciting for a young lad. It took Grandad a long time to work out what he could possibly be talking about when I asked him what Santa was going to bring him. He tried describing it, but the concept was as alien to me as refrigerators to headhunters (Grandad's reading a book about David Attenborough's early travels). So, as you can imagine, one was very intrigued to see what it was. One had taken the package from the lovely Amazon people who keep bringing prezzies (does one have to pay for these by the way?) and it was reassuringly heavy and chunky.

Anyhow, Christmas morning arrived and it was time to go next door and wish Merry Christmas and distribute gifts. Finally, all was clear, albeit pretty a-maz-ing. It was a "Hoverboard"; to give it its full title: A self-balancing electric scooter. It is the kind of machine (not a toy) that you wish you could be Callum's age again!

 What does it do? It has a rechargeable battery. You stand on it (takes a bit of practice I imagine, but I only saw Callum having already mastered it) and the wheels light up with flashing lights. Then, with no apparent effort on the rider's part, off it goes at a fair lick. It will turn on its own axis and go in reverse as well as forward. But that's not all! There is also a go-kart that you can fasten it onto. That needs more space because it goes speedily, controlled by a couple of handles.

Daniel got electronic game controllers and games for Christmas. Unfortunately, Grandad has absolutely no clue about their special features so, sorry readers, you'll have to ask Dan for more details of those. Aimee of course looked after her Nancy (pony) with special treats on Christmas morning and she is going to be very lucky and have a new stable (Nancy, not Aimee) in the New Year—more of which next time.

Oh, I mustn't forget to talk about Pippa. She is a farm cat obtained for re-homing from the RSPCA. Her "papers" describe her as "feral" but that seems a bit insulting; anyhow, she has accommodation in our farm buildings and top-class (Grandad thought, expensive) nosh from a local supplier. She hides in her temporary enclosure under blankets so I can't show you a pic yet.

75: Bearing up

I've had a complaint. Bruno says that every month the Mag features a doggy blog from Sue. He wants his own blog. OK I said, tell me what to write.

Well I have to tell you that Bruno is not the most talkative of companions. He is certainly faithful and does not complain when I put my feet on him (which I do most nights, whilst watching TV especially Friday nights when there is a double-bill of Doc Martin which Grandad and Rosie make a point of watching, even if we have seen the episodes before, more than twice at least.) On a recent Zoom social meet-up his provenance was even recognised! There you go, Bruno, you're featured!

On to other pets. I promised you a picture of our "feral" puss, innocuously called Pippa. Her *raison d'être* is to catch or at least scare off the barn rats. I have had to resort to devious means to get a photo, namely an automatic wild-life camera. The pictures prove she exists; otherwise, she is very shy and not easily spotted. But she eats well and leaves appropriate offerings in the litter tray so that's more proof that all must be well. And rats have not been seen for weeks.

I haven't said much about Nancy in these missives. Nancy is Aimee's lovely pony and one of her great virtues as far as Grandad is concerned is the fact that she produces plenty of fertiliser. He is amazed at how much she creates. (Grandad is musing now about the relative muck-production of cattle and equines *: I mean, you can easily see where the cattle have been, but have you tried weighing a cow pat?

Anyhow, Nancy has got a house—yes! It's a super thing and looks rather like my new tractor shed which one has invested in after fighting with a tarpaulin in the wind and rain for some years. (Tractor was evicted from her former lodgings when the farm buildings were converted.)

I am trying to get Callum (12 now) to share some of his culinary expertise with Mag readers. He has several fav. recipes. One of them is "spicy rice" which I think he has invented, and Mum assures me he is a dab hand at other meals. Watch this space!

*Cow 65 lbs dung per day, horse 35-45 lbs. The fertiliser values are about the same. Online is a fun website all about cow pats. Google has not told me what a single cow pat weighs, yet. I will have to do some field research.

76. Twistin' the night away

It was to be another fun evening at Grandma's and Grandad's. The headline act (of course, see previous articles) was to be PIZZAS. Grandad thought he had a genius idea, in order to ring the changes a bit from purchasing at that well-known Market Drayton darts shop, or some other pub game: the children could design their own! Pizza bases duly purchased, along with tomato and cheese. Callum particularly likes salami so of course there was plenty of that. Everyone else had margheritas. That seemed to go OK. What next?

Ellie had bought a game for them to play. It was "Twister". To be quite honest, G/dad thought this was well out of fashion, prehistoric even. But no, they all contorted themselves into the game with relish. As a variant, they had quiz questions. (Available on their smart phones.) Grandad was appointed quiz master. Grandma was in charge of throwing the dice to see which limb to move to which colour. They played with relish (well, actually, Callum got a bit fed-up and played with his virtual reality head-set. If any reader can explain this technology, please let Grandad know) for quite a while.

Then it was film time. They just love inventing dramas and acting them out whilst Charlotte films them on our video-camera. They they watch the result, along with previous productions. Grandad never imagined they would get such value out of his video-cam. They watch them over and over. Great nostalgia!

I promised you a photo of Bruno last month. Here you go. He'd managed to get out onto the patio. Naughty Bruno.

77: Animals doing their own thing

BANG CRASH CLANG. "What on earth is that noise?" asks a Blore Heath resident. "It's Mrs Editor scaring off the rabbits from the bottom of the garden. She's banging a ladle on a metal plate," was the answer.

A small colony of rabbits has indeed begun establishing their home at the bottom our garden in full sight, unwisely, of Rosie. Cheekily, they have dug a burrow slap bang in the middle of her treasured round bed; and they can be seen besporting themselves amongst the daffodils and—if you please– eating them! It is not that Rosie has anything against rabbits *per se* but (a) she does not want them to be eating the plants, (b) not burrowing in and under the lawn and (c) why come in our garden when there is a 25-acre field the other side of the hedge?

If you have read page my little essay on synchronicity of an earlier issue of the Magazine, you will be amused (?) to be told that, after trying to get Grandad to DO something about the rabbits (shoot them?-no), one opened the glossy catalogue of items that you never knew you needed until you saw them advertised [put your own hyphens in] that fell out of the Sunday supplement only to see advertised THE VERY THING Rosie was looking for! It is a solar-powered gadget that emits an ultra-sonic boom or similar and scares unwanted pests away. [Go then—ask me how you know it's working if you cannot hear it—good question.] Anyway, I have ordered it, confident in the knowledge that, before it arrives, they will have decided to go elsewhere, which phenomenon ought to have a name. (This is exactly what has happened!)

Nancy (Aimee's pony) cannot be allowed to eat rich grass or she goes lame. So she is on a restricted diet. But there is lush nosh all around, particularly in the garden which adjoins her paddock. New raised beds were being installed. Watching her chance, Nancy simply followed one of the consignment-bearers of wooden sleepers in, before the gate could be closed. Boy, did Nancy enjoy cropping the grass! But that was nothing to watching her when, finally, she was tempted back into her paddock. She ran round, a hyperactive mad thing, for half an hour—she had gorged on the human equivalent of several Mars Bars—a massive sugar hit!

We have a resident hare. What he or she is doing we don't really know, but s(he) has been around for weeks now. Looking for love? Or just a "mad" March hare? I'll keep you posted.

With all the rain our pond has become a little lake and we love to see ducks swimming around. There are also daffodils nearby, to wander amongst, lonely as a cloud.

78: Smore?

I'm writing this in the middle of a stupendous period of hot weather at the beginning of June. One was even inspired to rise at just after dawn (-ish, 5 am) and get out there in the veg patch to see if any weeds had escaped my evil hoe.*

We always enjoy a barbeque with Ellie and Charlotte and parents, who live opposite; it's all of 12 strides, door to door, so parking isn't a problem. "Come over later for a BBQ" - we don't need to be asked twice!

Becky always puts on a splendid spread, and we brought some asparagus and new potatoes. New spuds in late May? You are probably asking yourself? Well, they are very popular chez nous so I make sure I dig out any old bucket or container I can in January/February and pop 2 or 3 early spud tubers in, with sifted compost from the heap. (Digression: I got the tractor out yesterday to turn the heap, yes I know one should not boast about the size of one's compost heap, but it's easier to have a big one and then it justifies having the tractor, and especially if there is muck available.) They are still not very big but oh so tasty, with mint.

Towards the end of the meal, when HOME MADE ICE CREAM was being served (Becky again), out came marshmallows and, wait for it, a pack of choc digestives (plain). The children have always enjoyed toasting marshmallows on a BBQ or camp fire since they were little, and Callum was expert at toasting cocktail sausages ditto, but I was more than puzzled at the chocolate digestives.

Soon, all was clear, if surprising. A toasted marshmallow or two was sandwiched between two choccy biccies and scoffed with enthusiastic delight. Several trips to and from the table to the BBQ (Matthew even put fresh charcoal on to keep the heat going), the marshmallows were gone, and the choccy biccies depleted. The adults did not partake of this apparent treat; I think it needs a youthful palate.

"Smore"? It's the name for this culinary creation of choc bix and toasted marshmallow. Probably a corruption of "Would you like some more?" - "S'more?"

*I am being wotsit, the plot is replete with a diversity of native herbage.

79: BBQ time again, and work experience for Charlotte

The lovely weather has been great for barbeques once again and we've been lucky to be invited opposite *chez* Charlotte and Ellie and, next door *chez* Aimee, Callum, and Daniel for same.

Ellie, apart from schoolwork, told us that she is learning some new dances. It will be a delight to have a performance in due course. She entertained us with riddles, like "A plane crashed into a building with 1000 people in it. 102 people died. Where did they bury the survivors?" Grandad didn't get it for a while!

Callum enjoys cooking. One of his specialities is grilled halloumi cheese, to go with the usual burgers and sausages and salads. He also loves his creation, "Spicy Rice" which I hope to get the recipe for soon to share with you all.

Aimee is getting more confident on her pony (Nancy) and we watched her going round the paddock faster and faster and JUMPING over a low "fence" under the watchful eye of her teacher. Grandad thought he noticed that the pony, trotting (cantering?) not walking, leaned into the turn as she rounded the corner of the paddock (as on a bike) so obviously the rider must do that too—or could topple off. (Worth remembering in case Grandad decides to take up riding as he has only ridden horses so far in a straight-ish lines, slowly.)

Of course, the boys are keen on their electronic gadgets: Daniel appeared to be watching endless football which, it being post-Euros, Grandad could not understand. It turned out it was a video game and he was controlling the player who had the ball. (That's as much as Grandad could understand: he wondered about how you could possibly control all the movements of the other players, not to mention the referee.)

Charlotte had to do work experience for a week from school. It was a great opportunity to host it at Keele University where Grandad works*. *Inter alia*, during the week she had a project to do from Prof. Nicky who is professor of neuropsychology. This entailed testing the memory-for-faces (her Dad was the guinea-pig) using professional neuropsychology tests. He did very well but a little bird told me that he was peeved when he had to draw a complicated geometric pattern from memory without having been warned, which of course was deliberate. At the end of the week we clapped loudly when C. gave a presentation about the week in the large lecture theatre of the Dorothy Hodgkin Building. It was special, because Grandad has given hundreds of lectures in this theatre over 52 years at Keele. She especially enjoyed the electronic light controller, which is admittedly good fun, and handled lights and slide (PowerPoint) controller expertly.

[* Not when you read this. Grandad will have retired!]

80: Turn, turn, turn

In the dim and distant past that is Grandad's memory bank, there lurked memories of a hula-hoop craze in the 1950s. Sure enough, a search online came up with a readable article from no less a credible source than the Washington Post. Written in 1977 it notes an upsurge of interest in hula hoops, but nothing like the craze in the '50s, when over a 100 million hoops sold worldwide in 6 months.

Hula hoops originated in Australia, made of bamboo and used for exercise. Someone gave one to a toy firm called "Wham-O". It sat around in the office for months because no-one knew what it was for. Then a visitor chanced by and gave a demonstration to the boss. Showing it to his wife, she was shocked and said it was obscene. But three months later she was doing demonstrations!

The Washington Post at the time urged caution warning: "persons of mature years" [see below!] of "possible physical perils in hooping", concluding: "So our earnest advice is to leave the Hula Hoops to those who know how to make them behave; and these seem to consist exclusively of little girls between the ages of 8 and 10."

Whilst our grandchildren Ellie and Charlotte are no longer "little girls", they definitely have the knack of hula hooping. Grandad has always assumed that you need plenty of hip action to make the hoop twirl around your waist. But, watching Charlotte and Ellie in action, they make the hoop spin round their midriffs with no apparent movement other than a gentle to-ing and fro-ing.

"Have a go, Grandad". Game for a laugh Grandad tried it (and it could help his midriff problem; as 10-year old Lara, great grand-daughter of "cousin Betty from Cornwall" queried the other week, "Are you having a baby, John?"). But it fell dismally to the floor after a couple of revolutions. More practice needed.

Charlotte is a champion at the hoop, able to keep it going for longer than any of her school chums, whilst Ellie got two hoops going at the same time the other day.

I'm off now to make one—just a length of plastic water pipe and some gaffer tape will do the trick.

81: Fore!

A perennial challenge. What to do with our Fantastic Five during the long holiday? One had the idea of golf. Why not? Well, as it turned out, a golfing session was going to be more complicated than one might have thought...

Years ago (many, many) Grandad went to the golf driving range near Keele University. You bought a bucket of balls and a club and could spend a happy hour or so bashing these balls into the green yonder. He even took some golf lessons to perfect his swing. Hah! The teacher said that golf was simple—you learned how to putt (knees together, bend them a bit, hold the putter firmly down the shaft, size up the shot and then bingo—down the ball will go). What could go wrong? Then you only needed to perfect your swing and the rest was easy. I don't know about you but I think those statements could have been easily referred to advertising standards for total misrepresentation.

Anyhow, off we traipsed to said golf driving range, Charlotte, Aimee, Ellie, Callum and Daniel, all wondering what the grandparents had in mind. Just one problem, said the professional there, we don't rent out clubs to children (adults ones too long). OK, could we just watch for a bit whilst people do their thing? Yes of course.

Well, things had got a tad more serious since one was last there. The bucket of balls idea was still there but you tip them into a hopper and then then come up one by one on a magical tee that rises on its own with a ball already loaded. Next, there are screens that record your swing and tell you where you are going wrong. The customers there were DEADLY SERIOUS. And probably did not take lightly to a crowd of onlookers—but we left soon.

Plan B—crazy golf at the Eccleshall Garden and Wildlife Centre. It was great fun although at least one hole was probably impossible as you had to get the ball onto a concrete hillock in exactly the right place and at the right speed or it just rolled down the other side. Favourite hole—bash the ball into a circular steel runway and it whizzed round and out. Grandad enjoyed that.

We have a new resident at Blore Heath! Heggie the Hedgehog! He or she was snapped on Grandad's new wildlife camera trap. Heggie is sleeping in a corner of our barn and comes out at night to eat the food we put out for our feral puss who lives there to scare the rats away. They don't seem to mind each other—or perhaps puss has already discovered that hedgehogs are pretty spiny. It's the first time in 50 years at Blore Heath that Grandad has seen a hedgehog. He or she is getting very portly, but that's probably OK if you are going to hibernate for months on end.

82: Duck, duck, duck - GOOSE

Our wedding anniversary coincides with other birthdays, and we all convened for a lovely meal, so good after lockdown. There was a generation gap. One end of the table were the oldies whilst at the other were the youngies. They love their pizzas purchased, if you have been following this series, from a well-known purveyor of same in Market Drayton. Us lot had super roast chicken and salads with enormous home-made chips (Grandad really likes chips). [If you speak to me nicely I will tell you where the BEST CHIPS I HAVE EVER TASTED can be found, although it is quite a long way away.]

After the meal we persons of more advanced years chatted away whilst the younger members of the family—spontaneously it seemed and without any planning—got down on the floor to play some games. Now, they are all well into their electronic gadgets, be they phones or computer games. So it was very refreshing and encouraging shall we say about the nature of the "upcoming generation" to see them playing really old-fashioned games. One was a variant on "cat and mouse" which we used to play in cubs.

How to play? The person who is "on" walks around the circle of players and taps each person on the shoulder saying duck, duck, duck, duck (an unpredictable number of times), and GOOSE. The GOOSE person then jumps up [this is obviously best played by young people] and chases the "on" person to get back to the place where the latter was sitting. Aimee was the best at this! Grandad excused himself [getting down isn't too bad but fellow oldies will know what happens or rather doesn't happen then…].

An outing was to the Eccleshall Garden Centre for eats and fun. There was a super swing which gave everyone (inc. Grandad) a lot of fun. It's big enough for adults and is made of a large tyre with netting (like a basket, to stop you falling through!). There was a bit of a project to see if it was possible to swing it right over the top. Grandad was one of the subjects of this experiment—five Grandchildren can push a swing pretty hard—but he had to abort as it was getting higher and higher and higher, thus frightening Grandad.

And making him air-sick.

83: Star!

No, not a Christmas star but a TV one. Guess Grandad's surprise when "Auntie" rang up and said that she (they?) would like me to appear on Countryfile. Wow! They were going to do a segment (you have to be in the know to know the jargon…) on the National Forest Llama Trekking centre near Burton on Trent. To link with another piece they were doing, they were looking for "an expert" to talk to camera on the "health benefits of walking with llamas". My name had been put forward as an "ecopsychologist" who would know about these things.

You might not be surprised to know that there is not an extensive scientific literature on this topic. In fact, Grandad has not been able to find a single article. So one panicked for a little while as to what to say with my "professional ecopsychologist" hat on. Ecopsychology by the way is the growing area of interest in understanding the human relationship with the natural world. But soon some ideas started to flow and I had a selection of possible answers to whatever the presenter would ask me.

The day duly arrived and we met with Ellie Harrison, one of the Countryfile presenters, two cameramen, a sound recordist and a director. They spent quite a while deciding how best to shoot me—not for my "best side" but for a more interesting viewer experience. They decided that Ellie and I should be hand feeding llamas whilst we talked. We did one "take" and then they said could we do it all again, for different camera angles. Then the conversation was all technical like "do a slomo" (of me putting my hand in the feed bucket) and taking it out again and "get a wide angle" and "drone shot".

It was slightly nerve-wracking to see how the final, edited version would come out. It was screened on Remembrance Sunday (2021) to link in with a feature on the National Remembrance Arboretum which is near to the llama farm. But people seemed to think it OK. Phew!

In the picture I'm with Ellie Harrison, Countryfile presenter, the llamas are Kevin on the left and Barack O'Llama on the right. The rather unprepossessing chair was holding the bucket of food that Ellie and I dipped into to hand feed the llamas. They ate quite daintily and did not bite.

84. Llamarama

Anna, who runs the Llama trekking centre in Burton on Trent, invited us all to go and see her herd and have a walk with them. I thought the

big black one ("Barack O'Llama") (picture, left) might have remembered me fondly after I fed him loads—and chatted to him—eye to eye—whilst being interviewed for "Countryfile" (see December diary) with Ellie Harrison, but if he did he showed no sign.

After a short talk, we were invited to feed the llamas by hand and then take a walk around the field, leading them on their snazzy halters.

Llamas have their own agendas on a walk, even around their own patch. They stop and investigate any kind of herbage, nibbling the slightest sign of greenery. And there is a boss one who likes to lead. (Grandad had him.)

After the walk we were treated to super cakes and drinks in Anna's wondrous log cabin whilst the llamas rested in their stables.

BREAKING NEWS: THE COLLECTED "DIARY OF A GRANDAD" WITH ALL EPISODES FROM 2013—2021 WILL BE AVAILABLE SOON IN PAPERBACK. [IT IS! YOU HAVE IT IN YOUR HAND!]

POEMS

1. Christmas poem

Charlotte

Christmas comes once a year.
That's when Santa gets on his gear.
We always have nice food.
We are usually in a good mood.
It sometimes starts to freeze.
You could have some cheese.
    Santa is very exciting.
Sometimes Santa is writing.
        We can have apple pie.
Oh time does fly!
I usually have a Christmas tree. You hardly get it for free!
YIPPEE!

November 2012
Charlotte was in Year 2 at Hugo Meynell School

2. The lovely tree

Charlotte

There was a lovely tree
    Which stood by the sea.

People walked by
    And then buzzed a fly

But nobody took notice day or night
    Whether it was raining or bright.

A bird didn't land
    Even if it's leaves sparkled like sand.

The tree was sad.

Then one day someone said:
    "Look at that beautiful tree!"

Now the tree wasn't sad.

The tree was always happy
    and was never sad again.

January 2013

98

3. Far away from here

Charlotte

Far away from here
Nowhere, nowhere near
Lay a fine egg.
One day, a man called Greg
Automatically said
"What is that doing there?
"It's as brown as a big bear!
"Why is it brown? I want to know!"
But then a wise man said,
    "Ohoho! It's a CHOCOLATE egg!"
A boy tried to get it for him to eat
But he had a lot of people to try to beat.
They hadn't a single clue
What they were going to do.
The wise man said, "Don't despair!"
    "COME ON! LET'S SHARE!"

I asked Charlotte to write me something for the Lenten edition of the 2013 Magazine. Thanks Charlotte! Talking about it with her mum Becky, she thinks the "wise man" is Jesus.

April 2013

4. Let's just sit and relax

Charlotte

Let's just sit and relax,
With the sun on our backs,
Have an ice cream in a cone,
You shouldn't moan,
About the boiling sun,
When you're having fun,
So let's just sit and relax.

THE END

June 2013

5. Farm noises

Charlotte

The mooing of the cow
The oinking in the pen
The meowing of the cat
And the clucking of the hen!

The woofing of the dog
The goat eating hay
The sheep saying baa
And the horse saying neigh!

The quacking of the duck
The rustling of the bush
The moving of the trees
And the farmer saying "Shush!"

The snoring of the animals
The patting of the rain
The darkness of the night
And the roaring of the plane.

The cat, the dog, the hen, the pig, the goat, the horse and the sheep
I wish they'd all be quiet because I need to get to sleep!

July 2013

6. The Tudor Street

Charlotte

Verse 1
Walking along the Tudor Street.
With itchy socks that tickle your feet.
Peckish peacocks that eat the scraps,
Puzzled old men looking at maps.

Verse 2
The big butcher, as strong as a gorilla,
Look at those arms, he's a great killer!
People throwing waste out of the door.
What a horrible squelch, look at the floor!

Verse 3
I can see some greedy geese
That are being turned into fleece
The whistling wind is like a knife,
A criminal thief losing his life.

Verse 4
The washing on the washing line,
Lots of rich people drinking wine.
Some pigeon pie and other food
Makes all the Tudors in happy mood!

Verse 5
The trees are swishing from side to side,
Like the sea's delighted tide.
What a lousy Tudor Street
Look at the state of my nice, clean feet!

December 2013

7. Christmas

Ellie

Ellie was in Year 1 at The Hugo Meynell School.

Christmas is fun
    because Santa's on the run.

He brings lots of toys
    for all the good girls and boys.

People put up their Christmas trees,
    While Santa crawls down the chimneys
    on his hands and knees.

Christmas is exciting
    Because people are doing delighting.

When Santa sees the snow
    It makes him go ho ho ho.

THE END

December 2013

8. The snake

Charlotte

The snake can be different colours
It slithers on the floor
He sneakily catches his prey
Then moves off to get some more.

Cold-blooded, sticky and careful,
Scaly, hissy and quiet,
The snake is really interesting.
I think I'll go off and buy it.

He's starting to get annoying
I wish I'd put him back.
But there's no way I'm doing that now,
There's forty more on the stack!

The snake's squishy as a cushion,
With a tongue out, quick as a flash,
Slimy snake is a clean, green bean.
Sorry, need to dash!

Sneaky snake with cold blood is careful,
He's as curly as a lizard's tale.
Snake is very flexible
He can slither right over the rail!

Oh no, where's he gone?
He cost a lot of money.
But I've thought of a better pet –
What about a bunny?

Charlotte was in Year 3, Hugo Meynell School, April 2014.
Charlotte tells me that the final verse was difficult - it was only when she was copying out
again that it came to her. (Ed.)

9. Easter

Charlotte

I asked Charlotte if she would write a poem for the Magazine about Easter.

Easter is a time to celebrate,
There isn't any time to snooze,
Come on everyone, dance around!
There's no time to lose!

People get Easter eggs
From their family and friends,
Come on, everyone, let's eat our eggs!
The fun never ends!

Let's go on a treasure hunt,
Look out for some sweets!
Come on, everyone,
Get out of your seats!

I'm sad that Easter's over,
But I had a great day.
I wrote this poem to remember what I did,
So Easter's here to stay!

Charlotte was in Year 3 at Hugo Meynell School

May 2014

10. April Fool's Day

Charlotte

It's the first of April
April Fool's Day
Watch out, you're gonna be fooled!
We've got tricks to play.

"Your top's inside out!"
"Your hair's turned blue!"
"There's pen on your face!"
There's a wasp on your shoe!"

It's twelve o'clock now,
There's no more tricks to do.
Or I'll be the fool.
Aagh! There's a wasp on my shoe!

Charlotte was in Year 3 at the Hugo Meynell School.
June 2014

11. How to be cool

Charlotte

Alexander Jason Wood,
The coolest kid, in the neighbourhood.
Find your skateboard, look for your cap.
Watch out for the baby, he's having a nap.
Get ready for take-off, with your sunglasses on.
Now do a countdown, three, two, one.
Zoom through town, a grin on your face,
"Move and make way, for the skateboard race!"
Accidentally roll over, in the deep sticky mud,
Then hear your Mum shout…
"ALEXANDER JASON WOOD!"

Charlotte explained that the poem suddenly came to her after hearing about somebody with the surname Wood.

July 2014

12. Cats and dogs

Ellie

Cats and dogs, they love logs
Cats like mice, they taste nice.
Dogs like bones and they try to get ice cream cones.
They always meow and woof together
They don't like it when there's rain in the weather.

July 2014

13. The mad moon man

Charlotte

There was a mad man who jumped to the moon
After eating a baboon.
He ate some of the moon
Thinking it was cheese
But unluckily he had allergies
To dust and it made him sneeze
He bit some off,
It made an extremely loud sound.
And that is why
THE MOON IS NOT EXACTLY ROUND!

July 2014

14. Trampolining terror

Ellie

Come on everyone, jump on the trampoline
    And jump to the trampolining beat.
TRAMPOLINING TERROR!
    Electric shocks coming through your socks.
(You don't like it when your finger gets stuck in the net.
You slip and hurt yourself when the trampoline gets wet.)
TRAMPOLINING TERROR!

September 2014

110

15. The spider

Charlotte

There was a little spider
    Sitting on a chair
Watching little children
    Jumping down the stairs

He was angry about his eight long legs
    Cross about his horrible hair
Why couldn't he join in all the fun?
    He wailed, "It's just not fair!"

Then one day he found a solution
    He jumped up in delight
He started to make a web
    To slide down all night.

This invention was a success
    To spiders across the land
Even spiders right next to the sea
    Spiders on the sand.

16. When I had a cold

Ellie

When I had a cold, my teeth were made of gold
    I had chicken pox, so I didn't put on my socks.
Mum decided to go to the shops, then a robber called the cops.
    A fire engine came because they thought there was a fire
Then someone had a flat tire.
    After that we went home.
Then I punched myself with a comb.

17. Grandparents

Ellie

Grandparents are fun
They like to play outside in the sun
They don't like to play outside when it is rainy
They like to write poems
They are ever so brainy

December 2014

18. Christmas

Charlotte

I just can't wait till Christmas,
When Santa wears white and red.
Every year he delivers our presents
When we're all tucked up in bed.

Let's buy a beautiful Christmas tree,
To put up and decorate.
I hope Santa sees it.
I really just can't wait.

December 2014

19. My mum says

Edden El-Hashahar and Charlotte Hegarty

My mum says
Telly's bad for your head
My mum would often also say,
Homework day is Saturday,
And if there's something that I like,
I have to pay!
She also says the
Internet closes at seven,
And I'll only get pocket money,
When I am eleven.

From: *The Big Brilliant Book of Stuff*
By Edden El-Hashahar and Charlotte Hegarty
(Privately published, 2012)

February 2015

20. The awful taste of medicine

Edden El-Hashahar and Charlotte Hegarty

The awful taste of medicine,
That sinks into your tummy,
You can't even do it by yourself,
You get given it by your Mummy!

Oh, the awful taste of medicine,
That sinks into your belly,
And if you have it,
People say you are not well enough to
watch the telly!

From: *The Big Brilliant Book* of Stuff
By Edden El-Hashahar and Charlotte Hegarty
(Privately published, 2012)

March 2015

21. Easter

Charlotte

Easter is a time to celebrate
With your family and your mates.
Gobbling chocolate, eating Easter Eggs,
Treasure hunting, running away with our legs,
But as well as smiling and being nice,
Easter's a time to remember Jesus Christ.

Charlotte asked your editor (Grandad!) if there was time to put a poem in for the Easter edition of the Magazine and sat down and wrote this lovely poem there and then.

April 2015

22. Willow the dog

Charlotte

Our regular contributor Charlotte H. wrote this month about the Blore Heath Farm new dog, Willow. Willow was then an 18-month old, energetic cocker spaniel, and black. Let her out and she runs across the field like an arrow from the bow. She is anxious to please and generally wonderful.

Willow, Willow, Willow
She is as soft as a pillow.
Almost completely black,
But don't roll her ball, she won't give it back.

Willow, Willow, Willow
She is as soft as a pillow.
Very energetic,
If you throw her a toy, she'll go hectic.

Willow, Willow, Willow
She is as soft as a pillow.
Tongue as pink as a pig.
She's only eighteen months old, not very big.

Willow, Willow, Willow
She is as soft as a pillow.
If you see her jumping up,
Don't be scared, she's just a pup.

May 2015

118

23. Fire

Charlotte

Charlotte wrote this when she found out about the opening of the new Loggerheads fire station.

A little fiery spark,
Can light up a whole room in the dark,
It will give you warmth, it will give you heat,
It might also cook you something to eat,
The little spark will turn into a fire,
And grow higher and higher and higher,
It's very dangerous, it will burn all wood,
And probably anything else it could.
If you're not quick enough, everything will be ash,
And your house will be gone as quick as a flash.
"Bring in the fire engine as quick as you can!
My house is burning down, help me fireman!"
The firemen came and put out the fire straight away,
Thanks to the new fire station, they were the heroes of the day!

July 2015

24. The Earth's creation

Charlotte

Charlotte was in Y3 at Hugo Meynell. She told me that she wrote the poem because she did a lesson on the topic in school. She then had to write a poem about the things she had just learned.

On Day One, God created dark and light,
He separated day and night,

On the second day God split the sea and the sky,
He made sure the sea was down low and the sky was up high,

On the third day God created land,
He put on it grass, trees, flowers and sand,

On the fourth day God created two big lights,
The sun to shine at day and the moon to shine at night,

On Day Five he put in the sea fish and other creatures,
In the sky he put birds with wings as their main features,

On the sixth day God filled the Earth,
With lots of animals who would soon give birth,

Then he made boys and girls,
Boys with short hair and girls with curls,

On Day Seven God had a rest,
So on Sunday people go to church to be blessed.

August 2015

25. Llandudno!

Ellie

My dream is to find my destination and to find my inner peace.
When I find my destination it will be all up to me.
We might even go to the beach and I'm sure you'll all agree.
We might look for shells or jelly fish.
We might get an ice cream or some fish and chips.
We might play in the sun and have some great fun.
Everyone is really excited.
So if you want to come you can because EVERYONE IS INVITED.
There is no need to be moody
When you are watching Punch and Judy!
Now it's the end of the song.
I'm just saying Good Bye cos I'm moving on.
But good luck with the beach if you are going.
Good Bye!

Ellie was in Year 3 at Hugo Meynell.
(I want to go to Llandudno now! Grandad.)

26. The Battle of Blore Heath

Charlotte

The Battle of Blore Heath,
The year 1459,
Thousands of soldiers preparing for battle,
All standing in a line,

The nervous Lancastrians and Yorkists,
Got ready for the fight,
Then the battle began and forwards they ran,
Terrified at the sight,

Weapons and shields and men,
Were lying everywhere,
Thousands of people were shooting arrows,
Which were flying through the air,

The nasty, horrible scene,
Meant nobody was calm,
But who knew six hundred years later,
There would be a lovely farm?

October 2015

The Battle of Blore Heath was fought on September 23, 1459, making this year (2015) the 556th anniversary. Find out lots more about the Battle at the website dedicated to it - www.bloreheath.org - and search on YouTube for video clips taken at the various re-enactments held at Blore Heath Farm.

27. Cafe Des Gusting

Charlotte Hegarty

Don't go to that cafe,
The one down the street,
The cushions are hard,
And smell of feet.

The tables are weak,
And the chairs are big rocks,
They put vinegar on everything,
And serve fluff with fox.

The sausages are always
Out of date,
It takes an hour to cook,
It's not worth the wait!

But the reason people
Queue to get in,
Is to see Monsieur Gusting's
Unusually large chin!

Charlotte was in Year 4 at Hugo Meynell School
December 2015

28. Bathtime

Ellie

Before you get into the bath you have to strip
To check the temperature of the water just take a dip

Not stopping
Bubbles popping

Splish splash plip plop
Before it overflows make it stop

If you want to be an explorer
You have to get wet and go under the water

Chitter chatter in the bath
Whilst Dad goes to work and says "Must dash".

Ellie was in Year 3 at the Hugo Meynell School
December 2015

29. Crazy dances

Ellie

Some dances are really crazy
>You can't just sit around being lazy
You can't stand there saying just baa baa baa
>Wait - there's a chimp doing the cha cha cha
If you were doing ballet or tap
>You could do it wearing a baseball cap.

January 2016

30. The monstrous vending machine

Charlotte

The monstrous vending machine,
Fools everyone with his looks,
The second you insert the money,
You know you're a little bit stuck!

No one really notices,
The people that disappear,
It happens very gradually,
It's as if they were never here!

His technique is foolproof,
And extremely clever,
But eventually he must realise,
It isn't going to last forever!

An athlete came to the machine one day,
And decided to buy some sweets,
The monstrous machine grinned to himself,
He knew he was in for a treat!

The athlete fell into the trap,
As soon as the money went through the slot,
The vending machine chewed and chewed,
But the effort was a lot!

It was too much for the vending machine,
And he broke down,
All of the victims fell out,
And everyone was back in town!

Charlotte wrote this in year 5 at Hugo Meynell
January 2016

31. CHRISTMAS!!

Charlotte Hegarty, Charlotte Temperton, Mea Pickerill and Tom Gleave

The authors help out as Junior Assistants at Ashley Beaver Scout Meetings and wrote this, and read it out, for the final Beaver meeting of 2015, when we had a super Camp Fire [= traditional songs and home-grown entertainment around a campfire, on this occasion a pile of logs and artificial "flames"]. I love "Rudolf's nose gleaming in the night, lighting up the gloominess in sight".

Baubles hanging from the tree
What an awesome sight to see
On top of the tree you will find a star
The Wise Men followed it from afar.

Stockings hanging on the wall
What they contain brings happiness for all
Presents lying on the floor
The surprise is right behind the door.

Blizzards of snow in the air
You might even find it in your hair
Rudolf's nose gleaming in the night
Lighting up the gloominess in sight.

Feasting on the delicious food
Putting everyone in the mood
Finally Christmas is in the past.
A new year is approaching fast!

February 2016

32. Colds

Ellie

If you have a cold it is not very nice
Like if you have chicken pox or even head lice
If you have a cold you have to stay in bed all day
You'll have to go to the doctor's to make it go away
"Don't play music until you get a headache
Don't jump on your bed until it breaks......"

March 2016

33. A sunny Winter's day

Charlotte

Charlotte dedicates this poem "to all of my family"

Blowing grass glistens in the wind,
Cold air bites my cheeks,
Blotches of white in the clear blue sky
Leave gaps for the sun to take a peek.

I looked ahead at the horizon,
A pleasant smile spread across my face
Could you tell a storm was here last night?
Gertrude [1] didn't leave a trace.

"What happened to the weather?" I asked.
"Has the rain gone to bed?"
"No" came a voice
"It's nearly Spring" she said.

[1] *Storm 'Gertrude', January 2016*

34. BORING!

Ellie

Some things are boring.
Some things are not.
Some things are in the middle -
There is quite a lot.

Adults can be boring -
Some adults are.
But once they get into it,
They go too far.

There is a magician
But he's too boring.
By the time he's done
Everyone's yawning.

March 2016

35. The fashion designer

Charlotte

A fashion designer with lots of clothes,
Had a mansion near to here,
Her crammed wardrobe was as big as a room,
But then designing was her career!

There was a certain problem,
Which was deciding what to wear,
"Do I wear the lilac dress,
Or the '70s style flares?"

The butler saw no solution,
And the maids had not a clue,
So she went to see the Wise Old Owl,
Who knew just what to do,

"A smile will cheer people up more,
Than perhaps a beautiful dress,
So wear a smile on your face,
Even if your clothes are a mess!"

April 2016

36. What a scene!

Charlotte

It's chaos in the theatre
Just an hour to go
Before the curtains rise
And soon begins the show!

The actors and actresses are nervous
Determined to do their best
They try to be organised and ready
But oh no! The fairy still needs to get dressed!

High expectations from the audience
Celebrities sit themselves down
Front row tickets have gone in a millisecond
People must have seen the adverts in town!

A few more minutes left
The countdown lasts for an age
But finally, the director hisses "Action"
And the performance hits the stage.

June 2016

37. PRINCESS BLOSSOM ("Somewhere out of this world")

Charlotte and Ellie

The story of Rapunzel is revisited by our staff poets Charlotte and Ellie Hegarty in this month's poetry corner, which they wrote as a song.

Every night I'm just dreaming
It's harder than it's seeming
Just watching the sun go up
Somewhere out of this world.

I'm trapped in this deep dark tower
Boredom is blinding me
As I watch the hours
Somewhere out of this world.

Evilness surrounds my mum
I'm not sure she's real
My lizard is my company
He knows how lonely I feel,
Somewhere out of this world.

I'm trapped in this deep dark tower
Boredom is blinding me
As I watch the hours
Somewhere out of this world.

No fire exits, no escape
I'm waiting for my prince
To come in his red cape,
Somewhere out of this world.

August 2016

38. The story of Joseph and his coat

Charlotte

1. Jacob had a dozen sons and four wives,
        They all wanted Jacob in their lives,
   But Jacob had eyes for Rachel and no other,
        Her son Joseph was marked as the special brother.

2. Jacob had a multi-coloured coat,
        He gave it to Joseph to promote,
   The fact that Joseph was the best, or so it seems,
        But he shone because he could interpret any dreams,

3. The brothers got fed up with Joseph and his ways
        So they sold him off to Egypt to be a slave,
   His master liked him and so did his wife,
        Which made it easier for him to live his life.

4. Mrs Potiphar waited until he was alone,
        Suddenly he felt her scarf and he turned to stone,
   Potiphar the master, was on the trail,
        He saw Joseph with his wife and sent him to jail.

5. Pharaoh had had a bad dream,
   He sent for Joseph who knew what it could mean,
   "Seven years of lots of food to eat,
   Followed by seven years of famine, no corn or meat."

6. Joseph was in charge of the famine,
        Because he was good at forward planning,
   He stored up lots of food, so when the famine came through,
        He had enough to eat, so knew just what to do.

7. Back in Canaan, the brothers were hungry and weak,
        They had eaten all the food and had no sheep,
   So they set of to Egypt in search of some corn,
        They stepped across the Egyptian plains, looking white and drawn.

8. They begged Joseph, not knowing it was him,
        Joseph saw they were tired and getting slim,
   He gave them their food and went round the back,
        Slipped a golden cup into Benjamin's sack.

134

9. The brothers were shocked that he was a thief,
    They stared at him in dismay and disbelief,
Joseph knew now that they were good and true,
    He took off his hat and they said, "Is it you?"

10. Joseph saw his father again,
    He gave him a hug, when,
He realised that the love had multiplied,
    The brothers were watching on the side.

October 2016

39. Running in mud

Charlotte

There's a nightmare that I'm stuck in,
And I can't get out,
I'm running in mud,
That's drowning me out.

As fast as I can go,
My feet are whizzing round.
It changes nothing,
So my heart starts to pound.

I'm sinking deeper,
Down goes my neck,
Will it stop,
This everlasting trek?

My whole body feels sore,
No stopping for a minute,
As a nightmare, this is bad,
But worse, I'm stuck in it!

November 2016

40. This noisy street

Charlotte

There's people bustling,
Handbags rustling,
On this noisy street.

The shops are full,
The queues are dull,
With the sound of shuffling feet.

People talking,
People walking,
Grabbing a bite to eat.

Tall street lights,
In the dark, cold nights,
Standing in rows bright and neat.

Day in, day out,
There's always things to talk about,
On this noisy street!

February 2017

41. I LOVE DANCE

Ellie

1. Dance, dance, dance -
I love dance
And all you have to do is just
Prance, prance, prance.

2. If you practice
You will be great
But only if you eat
Everything on your dinner plate.

3. Some dances could be - soft like a pillow
Or sharp like a knife
But if you give it a go
It could change your life.

4. And you can choose
Any song
If the song goes with your dance,
You can't go wrong.

5. And please, please practice,
I really must implore you.
And if you're asking - I don't need to ...
'Cause I started way before you.

February 2017

42. A secret recipe

Charlotte

I knew a witch who lived far away,
I even went to her house one day,
She told me of a powerful spell,
It could make bad things become well.

This is how the recipe goes,
(Please make sure nobody knows)
Recite it in your head for about a day,
To make sure the memory will never go away.

Grab a cauldron - any size,
Wash it in water and wait until it dries,
Once you have cleaned up all the grime,
Add in a barrel full of slime.

Rats' tails and pigs' eyes are next on the list,
Then stir it all in with your fist,
Pour in a little water and then boil it,
(Leaving time to go to the toilet).

Finally, you need to grind,
All the dust and stone you can find,
Throw it all in; it should turn green,
The brightest colour you've ever seen.

Good luck and I hope it works,
You never know where evil lurks,
Keep this mixture always close,
You just don't know when you'll need it most.

Love from Charlotte

April 2017

43. Houston, we have a problem!

Charlotte

There is a lost connection
Listen you NASA lads
Send me the best collection
Of people we've ever had

Bring them down to HQ
From the left wing and the right
Better get a move on too
Or we could be here all night

Fix the wires; set them straight
Do what must be done
Come on now, it's getting late
We don't have time for fun

Oh, look, we're back online
I can see his face
Thank goodness, he seems fine
I knew he'd make the race

Hang on, what's that noise
Hear it pop and pound
Something's being destroyed
Oh dear, we've lost the sound.

June 2017

44. Memory Lane

Charlotte

Days of joy and days of shame
All lost in a photo frame
Never to be visited again
Those old days in Memory Lane

In your mind by night, by day
Never going to fade away
Sometimes courage, sometimes strain
Those old days in Memory Lane

Following through the ups and downs
Bound to make you smile and frown
There to add to the memory train
Those old days in Memory Lane

Though they get foggy as you stroll through time
The good will always sparkle and shine
Memories to help you through the pain
Those old days in Memory Lane

Old memories mixed in with the new
They're all different to suit you
In the thunder, sun and rain
Are those old days in Memory Lane

June 2017

45. A magic land

Charlotte

Take me to your magic land
I'll do whatever you command
I will do whatever you say
If I can see your land some day

Take me to see your mythical beasts
Take me to parties and midnight feasts
Take me to see unicorn trails
And teach me all of the fairytales

If you take me to diamonds and gold
I will do whatever I'm told
So take me to your land of fun
Always bright and full of sun

Where there's no negativity
There's always nice activity
Your land is where I dream to be
To see fairy tales and fantasy

July 2017

46. MY CAT

Ellie

My cat is a cute cat but he's never around
When he is he makes a cute mee-owing sound.

My cat is so fluffy and black and white
Two seconds later he's out of sight.

July 2017

47. SCHOOL NOISES

Charlotte

Stomp, stomp
  Children coming through the door
Clip, clop
  Teacher down the corridor
Chatter, chatter
  Children talking during break
Scrape, scrape
  Caretaker gardening with the rake
Munch, munch
  Lunchtime in the dinner hall
Kick, kick
  Children playing with a ball
Ding, ding
  There's the bell
Uh-oh
  The teacher fell.

August 2017

48. ADAM and EVE

Charlotte

Charlotte was a junior leader on Faith Quest, the Benefice Holiday Club organised by Denise Keen and the Benefice Young Person's Team during July 2017. Charlotte wrote two poems to celebrate sessions 1 and 2 - the first of five sessions of games, songs, prayer and Bible study on Bible story from Genesis to Revelation.

Adam and Eve were God's creation
The Serpent led them into temptation
And ruined God's plan
To make Woman and Man
Perfect across the Nation.

49. MOSES

Charlotte

Moses led the Israelites
Proudly with staff in hand
He fought Pharaoh for many years
To travel to the Promised Land.

With God's help, he freed the slaves
It took locusts, frogs and blood.
Then they travelled for forty years
In the hope that things would be good.

God provided food and drink
Moses passed away
The people arrived at the Promised Land
That is still there today.

August 2017

50. The chill in the night

Charlotte

She tiptoed across the landing. The clock in the living room struck quarter to midnight and Emma was getting her torch from the kitchen. After what seemed like forever, she reached the stairs and let out a huge sigh of relief. The coast was clear. Could she make it downstairs? She slowly, but cautiously, made her way down the cold, wooden steps. She began to relax as the bottom came nearer and Emma forgot all about the twelfth step, the creaky one. CREAK! She held her breath, hoping that no one, or nothing, had heard her.

Once she was absolutely certain that she hadn't been heard, she continued onto the thirteenth step. The clock in the living room struck twelve. Suddenly, she felt something cold rush through her and the world started to spin. She heard shrieking all around her and high-pitched voices were screaming "HURRY UP!" down her ear. An icy, bony hand gripped her shoulder and she fell to the ground, unconscious. Silence.

Just then, she opened her eyes, sweating all over. Her mum stood in front of her with her hand on Emma's shoulder and said, "Wake up! You're going to be late for school!

October 2017

51. An epic spell

Ellie

Ellie wrote a spell as part of her schoolwork at Hugo for English.

I'll add the slightest touch of a fly's wings
And a leaf from the tree where the blue bird sings
A green frog's pink tongue or a lizard's tail so long
I'll put in the smell of a lavender seed
And some slimy, sticky seaweed.

Will she get ill?
Will she get sick?
If she does, get away quick!

In the tree where the robin sang
Will she look up to the stars?
Will she fly all the way to Mars?
Will she go play with boring ball?
Or go smashing things through the wall?
Will she turn into a frog on a log Jumping into a bog?

Will she explode like a TNT toad?

November 2017

52. The Arctic

Charlotte

Gleaming snow and icy air,
Silence hovers all around,
Polar bears are on the prowl,
But without a sound.

Icebergs dominate the cold, cold water,
Sturdy, silent and tall,
But in all their modesty, they rule the land,
Making no noise at all.

The fish are hungry but surviving,
Away from the dangers of man,
But they always swim in the waters below,
As quietly as they can.

The Arctic is a beautiful place,
Of wonder, snow and fear,
There's lots to see and touch and smell,
But not much you can hear.

December 2017

53. De island

Ellie

De people are chattin.
De bloomin flowers in de golden sun.
De cloud in de sky is fluffy.
De children havin heap o fun.

De town is very loud.
De sweet corn pop.
De people walkin round.
De busy chip shop.

De sand is soft.
De sky is blue.
De children with ice creams.
De sprinkles just for you.

De vibrant hummin birds fly.
De mischievous monkeys shriek.
De squirrels runnin round.
De insects hard to seek.

De sweet smelling flowers.
De gentle, mild breeze.
De tasty berries growin.
De swayin palm trees.

December 2017

54. Sprucewood Cottage

Charlotte

The house stood gloomily in the night,
Crooked and in despair.
Years of storms had taken their toll,
The place was beyond repair.

The rain lashed down like a thousand knives,
The weak spruce barely stood.
Lightning sniggered, ready to strike,
As fast as it possibly could.

Thunderous clouds formed above,
In a shade of darkest grey.
They sent down their water in bullets of rage,
Determined to ruin the house by day.

And then one day, after decades of failure,
The weather had finally won.
The poor little cottage crumbled under the strain:
It had at last been outdone.

February 2018

55. Patience

(set in the future, from the perspective of a young girl, aged nine.)

Charlotte

Once there was a time when people were warm,
There was such a thing as seasons and sun was the norm,
Now it's winter every day,
The snow will never go away,
The cold has trapped us in.

Waiting, waiting, but spring will never come
Begging, begging, begging for the sun.

It's August, 4045, the Freeze ten years ago,
They say one day the ice will thaw but I think they don't know,
Downstairs the aerocars are dusty
The house has gone all musty
The cold has trapped us in.

Waiting, waiting, but spring will never come
Begging, begging, begging for the sun.

One day my snooze alert goes off and I stumble out of bed,
The wardrobe starts to pick my clothes; I ask it for dark red,
The curtains start to open, then Mum gives a scream,
Because some snow has disappeared and, wait, the ground is green!

June 2018

56. The wise old tree

Charlotte

The wise old tree
Stood proudly on a hill
Bursting with its knowledge
Yet ever so still

Taller than the rest of them
Older than time
Wiser than the universe
Its leaves would ever-shine

The other trees came and went
Day became night
But when the tree could shelter you
Everything was right

One day they came, their axes gleaming
Their beards bristly and tight
The lumberjacks came striding in
Ready for a fight

But however hard they might try
They could not cut the tree
It was too strong and wise for them
And so happy to be free

Many years passed on by
The tree was seen in awe
And stood so proudly on its hill
Rooted to the floor.

57. A leaf is a very exciting plant

Ellie

A leaf is a very exciting plant
It's small for a giraffe but big for an ant
It doesn't matter what you say
But whatever you do,
Don't blow it away.

A birch is a very exciting tree
It's small for a building but big for a bee
I don't care whether you frown
But whatever you do
Don't chop it down.

Litter is not an exciting thing
It ruins the world and every living thing
If you see some on the floor
Pick it up
Don't walk out the door.

Greenhouse gases pollute the atmosphere
If you are polluting, get into gear
Hurry up now, the world's on a clock
If you don't, you're in for a shock.

Plastic pollution is not good
Put it in the bin like you should
Do you really want the animals to die?
If you do, then I bid you GOODBYE

Our Earth is a very exciting world
Do you really want it shrivelled and curled?
If you don't, then shout and yelp
Our pretty world, the Earth, needs HELP.

Do you wanna help?
Oh, that's a relief
Everyone's entitled to their own belief
If you don't agree with what I've said
That's Okay, but the world is
DEAD!

February 2020

154

58. Watching the clock

Ellie

Watching the clock
Is like watching paint dry
I'm sitting here for some reason
But, sadly, I can't think why

What am I doing?
Why am I here?
It's all so very quiet
There is the ticking in my ear.

RING RING RING
"It's the fire alarm" I start to yell
Oh no, my mistake
It is just the school bell.

March 2020

59. At the football

Ellie

The panning of the camera
The cheering of the fans
They are making a racket
Like falling pots and pans

The kicking of the players
The bouncing of the ball
The game is just getting started
When the rain starts to fall

It is nearly half-time
And tension starts to rise
The game is so intense
I have to close my eyes

"What's going on I say?"
Because my eyes were shut
A player is shooting a penalty
I saw nothing but his foot.

March 2020

60. Limericks

LIMERICKS BY ELLIE HEGARTY

There once was a man called Ant
Who built his house on a slant
His furniture slid
Right on to his rib
I asked him to move but he can't.

I once met a girl called Lou
Who wanted to see how long she could chew
She chewed for DAYS
And never ceased to amaze
Now shes's made CHEWING the latest CRAZE.

RECIPES

1. RASPBERRY MERINGUE ROULADE

by Aimee

Ingredients:
5 medium egg whites
150g caster sugar
1 teaspoon corn four
500 ml (half pint) double cream
140g fresh or frozen raspberries

Method:

1. Preheat oven to 150c/300f/gas mark . Grease and line a 33 x 23cm (13 x 9in) Swiss roll tin with non – stick baking parchment.

2. Whisk egg whites until stiff, using an electric whisk. Add half the sugar and whisk until mixture is stiff and shiny. Add remaining sugar with corn flour and whisk thoroughly.

3. Spoon meringue mixture into tin and level surface. Bake for 40 - 45 minutes until firm to the touch. Leave to cool in tin for 1 hour, then turn out onto a sheet of baking parchment and peel away from backing.

4. For the filling, whip cream to soft peaks and gently fold in the raspberries. Spread the cream evenly over the meringue.

5. Roll meringue up from one of the short ends, then put on a plate with join facing down wards. Chill until needed: it keeps for 2 days in fridge. To serve decorate with raspberries and dust with icing sugar.

April, 2017

2. MERINGUES

Aimee and Ellie just love this recipe for meringues. Why not try it?

Ingredients:
4 egg whites
1/8 tsp salt
10oz (285 g) caster sugar
½ tsp vanilla or almond essence (optional)
8 fl oz (250ml) whipped cream (optional)

Method:
1. Preheat a 225f/110c/gas ¼ ovens. Grease and flour 2 large baking sheets.
2. With an electric mixer, beat the egg whites and salt in a very clean metal bowl on low speed. When they start to soft peaks, add half the sugar and continue beating until the mixture holds stiff peaks.
3. With a large metal spoon, fold in the remaining sugar and vanilla or almond essence, if using.
4. Pipe the meringue mixture or gently spoon it on the prepared sheet.
5. Bake for 2 hours. Turn off the oven. Loosen the meringues, invert, and set In another place on the sheets of prevent sticking. Leave in the oven as it cools.
6. Serve sandwiched with whipped cream, if wished.

May 2017

3. STRAWBERRY SHORTCAKES

Aimee

Makes 10 –

Ingredients for the shortcakes:
225g (8oz) self-raising flour   1 teaspoon of baking powder
50g (2oz) butter   caster sugar 25g (1oz) 1 medium egg
5 tablespoons of milk   ½ teaspoon of vanilla essence   Extra milk for brushing
For the filling: 225g (8oz) strawberries   150ml (1/4 pint) double or whipping cream

Method:
1. Heat the oven to 225c, 425F. Use a paper towel to wipe a little butter over a baking tray. 2. Sift the flour and baking powder into a big bowl. Cut the butter into chunks. Stir them into the flour.
3. Use the tips of your fingers and thumbs to pick up some butter and flour and squash and rub them together. Carry on doing this.
4. The lumps of butter will gradually get smaller and smaller. Keep on rubbing until they are the size of small breadcrumbs. Then stir in the sugar.
5. Break the egg into a cup. Add the milk and vanilla. Mix with a fork then pour into the big bowl. 6. Use a blunt knife to cut through the mixture again and again to mix it. It will cling together. Pat it into a ball with your hands.
7. Dust clean surface with flour. Put the dough on the flour. Roll over the dough turn it around and roll over it again until its 1cm (1/2 in) thick.
8. Cut out lots of rounds. Put them on the tray. Squash the scraps together, roll them out again and cut more rounds.
9. Brush a little milk onto each round. Bake for 10 – 12 minutes until risen and golden brown. Move to a wire rack t cool.
10. Remove the green stalks from the strawberries. Cut the strawberries into thin slices.
11. Whip the cream. Cut each shortcake in half.
12. Spread some cream on the lower half. Top with strawberry slices. Spread on more cream. Put the top halves back on.

June 2017

4. ROCKY ROAD BARS

Ellie and Aimee

Makes: 24 bars –

INGREDIENTS
Metric Cups 125 grams soft butter
300 grams best-quality dark chocolate (minimum 70% cocoa solids)
 broken into pieces
3 tablespoons golden syrup
200 grams rich tea biscuits
100 grams mini marshmallows
2 teaspoons icing sugar (for dusting)

METHOD

1. Melt the butter, chocolate and golden syrup in a heavy-based saucepan. Scoop out about 125ml / ½ cup of this melted mixture and put to one side.
2. Put the biscuits into a freezer bag and then bash them with a rolling pin. You are aiming for both crumbs and pieces of biscuits.
3. Fold the biscuit pieces and crumbs into the melted chocolate mixture in the saucepan, and then add the marshmallows.
4. Tip into a foil tray (24cm / 9-inch square); flatten as best you can with a spatula. Pour the reserved 125ml / ½ cup of melted chocolate mixture over the marshmallow mixture and smooth the top.
5. Refrigerate for about 2 hours or overnight.
6. Cut into 24 fingers and dust with icing sugar by pushing it gently through a tea strainer or small sieve.

5. TRIPLE CHOC COOKIES

Aimee

Makes 24 –

Ingredients:

125g unsalted butter, at room temperature.   100g caster sugar.
100g light brown muscovado sugar.   1 large free – range egg.
225g plain flour.   2 ½ tablespoons cocoa powder
½ teaspoon baking powder   ½ teaspoon bicarbonate of soda
A pinch of salt   100g plain chocolate chips   100g white chocolate chips
2-3 non-stick baking trays, ungreased

Method:
1.   Preheat the oven to 180c (350f) gas 4.
2.   Put the soft butter in the mixing bowl of an electric mixer. Add the caster sugar and brown sugar and beat with a wooden spoon or the whisk attachment until the mixture looks very soft and fluffy.
3.   Break the egg into a small bowl. Remove any pieces of shell then break up the egg with a fork. Add the egg to the mixing bowl and beat the mixture well.
4.   Set a sieve over the mixing bowl. Tip the flour, cocoa powder, baking powder, bicarbonate of soda and salt into the sieve then sift these ingredients into the bowl. Mix in with the wooden spoon, or with the electric mixer on low speed.
5.   Add all the chocolate chips to the bowl and mix in with a wooden spoon until everything is thoroughly combined.
6.   To make the mixture into cookies, dip your hands in cold water so they are just damp then take a small amount of the mixture – about a rounded teaspoon – and roll it into a ball. Set the ball on to the prepared baking tray, then make 23 more balls in the same way. Set the balls about 3 cm apart on the trays.
7.   Put the cookies in the preheated oven to bake for 15 minutes. Carefully remove the trays from the oven and leave to cool for 5 minutes before transferring the cookies to a wire rack. Leave to cool completely, then store in an airtight container. Eat your cookies within a week of baking them.

August 2017

6. EASY PIZZA

Aimee

Aimee's recipe this month is "eezee-peezey"! Just follow these simple steps to convert a humble baguette into a delicious meal!

Ingredients:

150g Tomato passata with basil,
Ciabatta bread
 250g mozzarella cheese
And toppings for your pizza.

Method:

1. Put the bread onto a chopping board and cut it in half along its length.
2. Put both halves onto a large baking tray.
3. Spread each piece of bread with the tomato mixture. Thinly slice the mozzarella cheese, and then lay the slices on top.
4. Add any toppings that you want for example cheese, pepperoni or ham, then if you want sprinkle a bit of parmesan cheese on top.
5. Bake the pizzas in the oven for about 15 minutes.
6. Lift the pizzas out of the oven and let them cool for five minutes.
7. Cut them up into pieces and eat them straight away.

September 2017

7. MARSHMALLOW SQUARES

Aimee and Ellie have worked together on this month's yummies

Ingredients:
250g (9 oz) marshmallows
2.5ml (1/2 tsp) vanilla extract
100g (3 ½ oz) butter, diced
175g (6 oz) rice krispies

Tools:
18x 28cm (7 x 11in) oblong tin
Saucepan
Wooden spoon
Metal spoon
Knife

Method:
1. Grease a 18 x 28 cm (7 x 11 in) oblong tin. Place 200g (7 oz) of the marshmallows, with the butter and vanilla extract in a medium saucepan.
2. Place over a medium heat and cook until the butter and marshmallows have melted. Roughly chop the remaining marshmallows.
3. Mix the toasted rice with the marshmallow mixture, then stir in the extra marshmallows. Spoon the mixture into the tray and press down with the back of a spoon.
4. Allow to cool in the tray and then cut into squares.
5. THEN EAT ITTTTTTTTTTTTTTT!!!!!!!!!!!!!!!!!

8. MILLIONAIRES SHORTBREAD

Aimee and Ellie

Makes 9-12 pieces -

This month, our catering team have sourced a massive favourite of theirs and indeed everyone's. So get the scales out and be a MILLIONAIRE!

INGREDIENTS

200g shortbread biscuits, crushed
25g butter, melted
150g dark brown soft sugar
397g can condensed milk
200g milk chocolate, melted

WHAT TO DO

1. Line 20cm square tin with baking paper.
2. Mix the crushed biscuits with the melted butter and then lightly press the mixture into the tin to make an even layer. Chill for 20 mins.
3. Place the butter and sugar into a saucepan and stir over a medium heat until the butter melts and sugar dissolves. To make a golden caramel, add the condensed milk, stirring continuously, until the first bubbles appear on the surface. Remove from the heat as soon as it comes to the boil.
4. Spread the caramel evenly over the crumb base and then cool and chill for about half an hour. Pour the melted chocolate over the caramel, smoothing to the edge.
5. When the chocolate has hardened a little, cut into squares

November 2017

9. GINGERBREAD BISCUITS

Your monthly recipe presented by Aimee and Ellie

MAKES 24

INGREDIENTS

175g/6oz plain flour,
¼ tsp bicarbonate of soda,
Pinch of salt,
1 tsp ground ginger,
1 tsp ground cinnamon,
65g/2 ½ oz unsalted butter, chopped,
75g/3oz caster sugar,
2 tbsp maple or golden syrup,
1 egg yolk, beaten,
White chocolate

METHOD
1. Sift together the flour, bicarbonate of soda, salt and spices into a large bowl. Rub the butter into the flour until the mixture resembles fine breadcrumbs.
2. Stir in the sugar, syrup and egg yolk, mix to a firm dough and knead lightly. Wrap (in Clingfilm) and chill for 30 minutes.
3. Preheat the oven to 180c/350f/gas 4. Grease two large baking sheets and roll out the gingerbread dough on a floured surface. Cut out the biscuits using floured 13cm/5in cookie cutter.
4. Transfer to the prepared baking sheets and bake for 10-15 minutes or until just beginning to colour around the edges. Leave on the baking sheets for 3 minutes and then transfer to wire rack.
5. Melt the white chocolate and drizzle over the biscuits, then leave to cool for 2 minutes.

Editor's taste-test verdict - *very acceptable with a cup of tea - light, crunchy and flavoursome and the drizzled white chocolate adds something special.*

10. CHOCOLATE TRUFFLES

Aimee and Ellie

INGREDIENTS

- 200g (7oz) milk chocolate
- 100ml (3.5floz double cream)
- 15g (0.5oz) unsalted butter
- a few drops of orange, vanilla or peppermint extract (optional)
To decorate:
- sifted cocoa powder
- grated milk, plain or white chocolate
- sprinkles
- chopped nuts

METHOD

1) Break the chocolate into small pieces in a medium sized bowl. Put the cream in a small saucepan with the butter and bring slowly to the boil.
2) Immediately pour the cream and butter mixture over the broken chocolate. With a wooden spoon stir until the mixture is smooth and all the chocolate has melted.
3) Stir in a few drops of orange, peppermint or vanilla extract if using. Cover and allow the mixture to cool for about 30 minutes at room temperature.
4) Chill in the fridge for about 2 hours and then using a teaspoon, scoop out bite-sized pieces. Dust your hand lightly with cocoa powder and roll into balls.
5) Immediately roll the truffles in sifted cocoa powder, grated chocolate, sprinkles or chopped nuts. Place in individual mini cup cases and chill. They will keep for up to 10 days.

THE EDITOR WRITES: A sample of these appeared the other day at the Editor's domicile. I can tell you they were absolutely scrummy. By all means spend your hard-earned pennies flying to Brussels for those famed Belgian chocolates, but how much better to make your own with this magic recipe! I am happy to sample any you make - just bring to church on a Sunday...

May 2018

11. CHOCOLATE MINI ROLLS

INGREDIENTS

30g cocoa powder / 15g butter, melted
½ tsp vanilla extract / 3 tbsp boiling water
3 large eggs, separated / 75g caster sugar
Filling:
75g butter, softened / 150g icing sugar / dash of double cream (optional)
Decoration
150g plain chocolate /150g milk chocolate /50g white chocolate

METHOD

1. Preheat the oven to 180°C/fan 160°C. Grease a Swiss roll tin, and line the base with greased baking paper.
2. Mix the cocoa powder, vanilla and boiling water together in a small bowl, forming a paste.
3. Whisk the egg yolks and 50g of the sugar until light and fluffy. In a separate bowl, whisk the egg whites until soft peaks form, adding the sugar until fully incorporated.
4. Mix together the chocolate mixture and the egg yolks, and fold in 1/3 of the egg whites. Fold the remainder of the egg whites in to make an airy batter.
5. Pour into a Swiss roll tin. Level out, being careful not to remove too much air from the mixture.
6. Bake for 12-18 mins, and place the tray onto a cooling rack, and cover with a damp tea towel to cool completely.
7. Beat the butter, gradually adding the icing sugar and continue to beat until white and fluffy. If the mixture is stiff it will be difficult to spread, so add a dash of double cream to soften the buttercream.
8. Turn the cooled cake out onto clean baking paper, and peel off the back. Score the cake a few centimetres in from the short ends.
9. Spread the buttercream across the top of the cake, working your way to the edges.
10. Roll from both of the short ends towards the centre and cut in between the two rolls. One end of mine rolled well, the other cracked and parts of the cake were stuck to the baking paper. Trim the ends and cut each roll into three even pieces. Place them seam down on a cooling rack and pop into the fridge to firm up.

11. Melt the milk and plain chocolate together over a bain marie. Place the cooling rack over a baking tray to catch extra chocolate, and pour it over the mini rolls, covering all sides, but leaving the base exposed.
12. Place back into the fridge to solidify whilst you melt the white chocolate. Drizzle the white chocolate over the mini rolls. We used a bottle with a nozzle,
13. *Watch them disappear.* [Ed.]

12. FRESH TOMATO & BASIL SOUP

Aimee and Ellie

- Serves 4-5
- Preparation time: 35 minutes + 30 minutes cooking

INGREDIENTS
50g (2oz butter or 30ml (2 tablespoons) oil
6 shallots, chopped
1 garlic clove, crushed or chopped
30ml (2 tablespoons) plain flour
850ml (1.5 pints) chicken stock
900g (2lb) beef tomatoes, skinned and chopped roughly
30ml (2 tablespoons) tomato puree
45ml (3 tablespoons) chopped fresh basil
salt and freshly ground black pepper
chopped fresh basil to garnish

METHOD

1. Heat the butter or oil in a large saucepan and cook the shallots and garlic for 3 minutes, stirring occasionally.
2. Add the flour and cook for 1 minute, stirring all the time.
3. Gradually add the stock and bring to the boil, stirring all the time until thickened.
4. Stir in the tomatoes, tomato puree and fresh basil, season well; cover and simmer for 30 minutes.
5. Cool slightly and then puree until smooth. Reheat and serve garnished with more chopped basil.

July 2018

13. PIZZA SQUARES

Ellie and Aimee

INGREDIENTS
Dough:
2.5ml (1/2 tsp) caster sugar
5ml (1 tsp) active dried yeast
350ml (12 floz) lukewarm water
5ml (1 tsp) salt
500g (1lb 2oz) strong white bread flour
15ml (1tbsp) olive oil
Tomato Sauce:
300ml (1/2 pt) passata
30ml (2tbsp) tomato puree
2.5ml (1/2 tsp) sugar
5ml (1tsp) dried mixed herbs
200g (7oz) grated mozzarella cheese

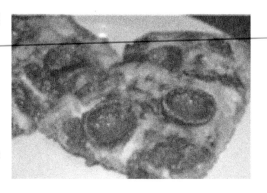

METHOD
1. Put the sugar, yeast and water in a bowl, mix and leave for 5 minutes. In another bowl, sift the flour and salt, then add the oil and the yeast mixture.
2. Stir with a knife to form a dough then knead for 4 to 5 minutes. Place in a bowl, cover with a clean damp cloth and leave in a warm place for 1 hour.
3. Meanwhile, make the tomato sauce. Place all the ingredients in a small pan and simmer gently for 5 minutes, allow to cool.
4. Preheat the oven to 220 degrees Celsius, 450 degrees Fahrenheit, gas mark 7. Using a floured hand, punch the dough to knock out the air, then knead lightly on a floured surface.
5. Divide the dough in half, then roll out each to a rectangle and place on a baking sheet. Spoon the tomato sauce over, then sprinkle with the cheese.
6. Add any other toppings you fancy and then bake for 15 minutes until golden. Cut in to squares and serve.

August 2018

172

14. COFFEE CAKE

Ellie and Aimee

INGREDIENTS
170g caster sugar - 170g butter
 or margarine, plus extra to grease
3 large eggs - 170g self-raising flour
1 ½ tsp baking powder
1 tbsp instant coffee (add more if you like it strong)
dissolved in 1 tbsp hot water
For the icing
225g icing sugar   100g butter or margarine
1 ½ tbsp instant coffee dissolved in 1 tbsp hot
water
strawberry jam (optional)   walnuts or cherries, to decorate (optional)

METHOD
1. Heat oven to 160C/140C fan/gas 3. Line and grease 2 x 18cm sandwich tins. Add the sugar and butter to a bowl and whisk until very fluffy and pale.
2. Whisk the eggs in a mug with a fork, then add them gradually to the mixture with 1 tbsp of flour each time. (Make sure you don't use all the flour.) When the eggs have been fully combined into the mix, add the rest of the flour and the baking powder and fold it in gently.
3. Add the dissolved coffee to the mixture, still folding. Divide into the sandwich tins and cook for 25-30 min until risen and firm and a skewer inserted into the middle comes out clean. Leave to cool in the tin for 5 mins then turn out onto a wire rack to cool completely. Can be frozen at this stage.
4. Meanwhile make the icing by beating the icing sugar with the butter until light and fluffy, then add the dissolved coffee. Whisk then cover and put to one side until ready to ice the cake.
5. Once the sponges have completely cooled, spread half the icing on the bottom of one (leaving around half for the top) and spread the strawberry jam on the bottom of the other, if using. Sandwich together, spread the remaining icing on top. Decorate with walnuts, or cherries if you prefer.

September 2018

15. HONEYCOMB ICE CREAM

Aimee and her cousin Amelia

INGREDIENTS
4 tablespoons golden syrup
150g caster sugar
2 teaspoons bicarbonate of soda
600ml double cream
397g (1 tin) full-fat condensed milk

METHOD

1. Put the syrup and sugar into a large deep saucepan and stir over a low heat until the sugar has dissolved and turned into a golden caramel colour.
2. Remove from the heat and tip in the bicarbonate of soda, stir until it is evenly incorporated and foaming. Then tip the honeycomb onto baking paper – do not touch it as it will be burning hot. Leave for about 20 minutes to cool and solidify.
3. Meanwhile whip the cream in a large bowl until it has soft peaks. Then pour in the condensed milk and stir to combine.
4. Now break the honeycomb into bite size pieces. Save a third of the honeycomb and fold the rest into the ice cream mixture.
5. Pour the ice cream mixture into a loaf tin lined with cling film, cover with more clingfilm and freeze for 6 hours or overnight.
6. Turn out onto a serving dish and top with the remaining honeycomb.

November 2018

16. CHOCOLATE MUFFINS

Callum

Callum says:
These are so good you cannot not make them!

225g plain flour
1 teaspoon bicarb
80g light brown sugar
2 eggs
125ml vegetable oil
100g white chocolate (broken into large chunks)
2 tablespoons golden syrup
1 teaspoon cocoa powder.

Callum says this is what you have to do:

1. Preheat the oven to 200c and line a muffin tin (should make 12)
2. Just bung the whole lot together into a large bowl (excluding the white chocolate) and mix it up until it looks like a lumpy mess
3. Add the chocolate chunks and then spoon into muffin cases… (I like to over-fill my muffin cases so I tend to get 10 muffins rather than 12)
4. Bake for 15 minutes until risen and cracked.
5. Eat and of course, enjoy!

Thanks to Callum for this recipe - yes, he really did make it himself and brought the muffins round for the Editor and Mrs Editor to enjoy!

Blore Heath Farm

TERTIUS INGPEN

Printed in Great Britain
by Amazon

79867460R00106